THE JEWISH PROPHET

VISIONARY WORDS FROM MOSES AND MIRIAM
TO HENRIETTA SZOLD AND A. J. HESCHEL

Featuring illuminated manuscripts from the British Library

RABBI DR. MICHAEL J. SHIRE

JEWISH LIGHTS Publishing

Woodstock, Vermont

For Marcia, the prophet in my life.

With thanks to Fiona Robertson and Cathy Herbert at Frances Lincoln for their dedication and skill, to the CJE staff for enabling me to take the time off to write, to Rabbi John Rayner and Asher Amir for casting their eye on the text, to the Rice University library in Houston for its superb Judaica collection and to the Plumb family's hospitality. Special mention to Anya, who slept while Abba wrote!

Published and distributed in the United States and Canada by Jewish Lights Publishing.

The Jewish Prophet:
Visionary Words from Moses and Miriam to Henrietta Szold and A. J. Heschel
Copyright © 2001 Frances Lincoln Limited
Original text copyright © 2001 Rabbi Dr. Michael J. Shire
Notes to the illustrations by Ilana Tahan copyright © 2001 Frances Lincoln Limited
All illustrations reproduced by the kind permission of The British Library © The British Library Board, 2002
The publishers are grateful to all the copyright holders who have given permission to reproduce work in this book. All reasonable effort has been made to trace copyright owners of quoted material, but the publishers would be happy to rectify any errors or omissions in future editions of this book.

The spelling of all words in this volume follows British style.

For information regarding permission to reprint material from this book, please write or fax your request to Jewish Lights Publishing, Permissions Department, at the address / fax number listed at the bottom of this page.

Library of Congress Cataloguing-in-Publication Data

The Jewish prophet : visionary words from Moses and Miriam to Henrietta Szold
and A. J. Heschel / edited by Michael Shire.
p. cm.
ISBN 1-58023-168-3
1. Prophecy—Judaism. 2. Jews—Biography. 3. Prophets—Biography. 4. Bible. O.T.—Biography.
5. Rabbinical literature—Translations into English. 6. Illumination of books and manuscripts.
7. British Library. I. Shire, Michael.
BM645.P67 J48 2001
296.3'1155—dc21

2001005905

Set in Baker Signet

Printed and bound in Singapore

10 9 8 7 6 5 4 3 2 1

Jewish Lights Publishing
A Division of LongHill Partners, Inc.
Sunset Farm Offices, Route 4, P.O. Box 237
Woodstock, VT 05091
Tel: (802) 457-4000 Fax: (802) 457-4004
www.jewishlights.com

CONTENTS

INTRODUCTION

The Jewish Prophet is a collection of portraits of individuals in Jewish history, ancient, medieval and modern, who have made a contribution to the prophetic role through the ages – a series of men and women who believed they were called to a special task in speaking God's word, and who served as the moral and spiritual leaders of their time. They acted as critics of the evils of society, rooted out corruption among those in power, and provided healing and comfort in times of despair and hardship. The prophet has often mistakenly been seen merely as a foreseer of the future. In fact, the prophets reviewed the past and looked through the present to the future, emphasizing that actions taken today will have consequences tomorrow. Abraham Joshua Heschel clarified this in his classic study of the prophets that 'the prophet's eye is directed towards the contemporary scene; the society and its conduct are the main theme of his speeches. Yet his ear is inclined to God.'

The word *prophet* is derived from the Greek *prophetes* meaning 'one that speaks forth'. The Greek translators of the Bible used the word *prophetes* to encompass various types of Hebrew prophet. These included the *hozeh* (visioner) and the *ro'eh* (seer). However, the most common title used in the Hebrew Bible is *navi*, meaning an appointed messenger of God who is charged with communicating God's will to the people. Often reluctant to take on the role but ultimately infused with a passionate commitment to seeing it through, the prophet becomes a radical individual answerable to no one except the divine moral authority that he or she represents. None of the named biblical prophets had any official role in ancient Israelite society, and they all had different backgrounds and positions in society. Each had their own style and retained their individuality, documented in the literary works that detailed their pronouncements, dreams and messages. Abraham Joshua Heschel said that 'the prophet is not a mouthpiece, but a person; not an instrument, but a partner, an associate of God'. Through the prophets, the divine message of moral law and social conscience was delivered. The *navi* or feminine *nevi'ah* was a man or woman of God, speaking God's will to the nation for the advancement of justice, peace and religious truth. The *navi* stood up against the establishment when kings and priests had become corrupted in their use of power. They protected the rights of individuals, especially the rights of those who were unable to defend themselves. As a consequence, the *navi* often had to suffer imprisonment, banishment or coercion to bend to the ruler's wishes. Compromise, however, was not in the nature of the *navi* and this distinguished false from true prophets.

The concept of the *navi* ended with the canonization of the Hebrew Bible in the fifth century BCE, and Jewish rabbinic tradition later

declared that prophecy had come to an end (Talmud Yoma 9b). Nonetheless, others in the Jewish tradition, notably the author of *Seder Olam Rabbah* in the second century CE and even Maimonides himself, understood prophecy to be ongoing, or with the potential to return whenever God should call again. The Jewish contribution to the search for truth and justice within a spiritual framework continued, and those who lived out a prophetic role after the biblical prophets share, in whole or in part, the characteristics of the *navi*. Individuals emerged who were passionate in their advocacy of social betterment or of radical change in times of oppression. They echoed the role of the ancient prophets by standing up against power, often at great personal danger, presenting the truth about the poor and dispossessed and calling out on behalf of those who had no voice. Though rooted in their own time and political reality, these medieval and modern *nevi'im* have given expression to sublime notions of freedom and justice. They call for individual liberty, democratic ideals and universal peace, ideas that have moulded the very nature of Western civilization and its political, social and religious ideals. In the sense that their truth is valid for all time and all places, they are said to prophesy the future. Through their inspirational words and poetry of passion, they continue to speak to us of their vision of a harmonious, free and spiritually rich world. Their voice speaks clearly, across the generations, in the timeless words of the biblical prophet: 'What does God require of you – only do justice, love mercy and walk humbly with your God' (Micah 6:8).

This compilation of textual sources of Jewish prophets, spanning over three thousand years, presents the lives and works of these individuals, recorded through their own voices as they express the need for social improvement and direct action, revealing some of the greatest

contributions that Judaism has made worldwide. Though rooted in the community and destiny of the Jewish people, the prophets have understood the mission of Israel to be a 'light to the nations' and have crystallized the moral law for all peoples.

Each of the men and women in this book has been described as a prophet by biographers or by the historians of their own time. Some may perceive this as a controversial appellation but I believe it has been used for these individuals because of the special category of holiness and direct action that they demonstrated. The number of pages restricts the selection, as more could be chosen who fit this category. Each one included here was, I believe, divinely inspired to dedicate their life to changing the world around them for the better. As Jewish prophets, they remain deeply embedded within their Jewish heritage and community, implementing the biblical ideals of prophetic Judaism, while also speaking and acting outside Judaism to a wider world. The accounts and words of these remarkable men and women remind us that there is a potential for us all to be prophetic, to respond to the divine call of conscience within us. In doing so, we assist in Judaism's sacred aim of actively promoting justice and goodness in the world.

IN THE BEGINNING

In the beginning, prophecy developed as an expression of the Hebrew spirit. It was born in, and preserved by, Israel and has burned steadily to illuminate humanity's path to redemption. Each week in synagogue, portions from the second section of the Hebrew Bible, the Prophets, are read as an additional scriptural reading, the Haftarah. The biblical prophets, from Moses to Samuel to the fifteen literary prophets, produced some of humanity's most sublime ethical treatises, spanning nine hundred years in an age of great turmoil and uncertainty during the rise and collapse of the Near Eastern empires. The first Jewish Commonwealth was established and fell in this time. Yohanan ben Zakkai and Akiva witnessed the second destruction of God's Temple and recurring exile from their Promised Land.

The prophets provided a voice of both warning and comfort to an embattled and dispirited people, encouraging them to trust in the destiny of moral rectitude and faithful commitment to God's Covenant with the Jewish people. They encountered the ridicule and persecution of those who despised change, particularly those who held power. However, God's word prevailed, sometimes predicting the future, but mostly warning and cajoling the people to listen to God and to the good in themselves.

> *It is too light a thing that you should be my servant to raise up the tribes of Jacob and to restore the offspring of Israel. I will give you for a light unto the nations that my salvation may be unto the end of the earth.* (ISAIAH 49:6)

MOSES
FOUNDER OF THE MORAL LAW
THIRTEENTH CENTURY BCE, SINAI

I have put before you life and death, blessing and curse.
Choose life, so that you and your offspring may live.
Love the Eternal one your God by heeding God's call
and being faithful to God.

(DEUTERONOMY 30:19–20)

The story of the prophets begins in the thirteenth century BCE with Moses, the greatest of them all. Called by God to take on the seemingly impossible task of delivering the Hebrew people from Egyptian slavery, the Bible relates that this giant of history was initially reluctant to tread such a dangerous and radical path. Like those who came after him, Moses neither sought his prophetic role nor, was he democratically elected to it by the people. It was by sheer force of the message he delivered that – in the face of vilification, threats and sometimes mortal danger – he succeeded in bringing together a disparate people to a distant mountain in the wilderness, and there enunciated the laws that were to underlie the teachings of all the prophets that followed.

As the adopted son of Pharaoh's daughter, Moses was raised apart from his own people. Powerless to intervene, he watched from the royal palaces as his fellow Hebrews suffered under the yoke of their Egyptian oppressors. His sense of injustice was irreversibly awakened, however, when as a young man he witnessed an Egyptian taskmaster viciously beating a Hebrew slave. Moses killed the Egyptian and fled to Midian (mainly in northwest Arabia) where he married Zipporah, daughter of the local priest, Jethro, and settled into life as a shepherd. Moses' vision of God at the burning bush in Midian marks the beginning of his time as prophet, prompting his return to Egypt to plead with the Pharaoh for his people's freedom. Ultimately successful, he led the Israelites out of Egypt across the Red Sea (*c.* 1250 BCE), and the wanderers began their long journey through the wilderness towards the Promised Land. At Mount Sinai, where Moses stayed for forty days, he received the Ten Commandments. He taught these and other laws to the people, thereby establishing the norms of Western civilization as we know it today.

Each of the biblical prophets was passionately driven to fulfil their divine task, but each was also mortal, with human failings and weaknesses. Moses fell short in God's eyes as he became exasperated with the people's stubbornness and sometimes lost faith in the mission he was called to serve. Yet, more than any who came after him, he was privileged in his intimate relationship with God: the Talmud (Yevamot 49b) remarks that while the other prophets saw God through a dim glass, Moses saw through a clear one. He served as an intermediary between God and the people until his death just outside the borders of the Promised Land, and is for ever remembered as a faithful servant of God and the founder of the moral law.

CALL TO PROPHECY

Now Moses, tending the flock of his
father-in-law Jethro, the priest of Midian,
drove the flock into the wilderness, and
came to Horeb, the mountain of God.
An angel of God appeared to him in a
blazing fire out of a bush.
He gazed, and there was a bush all aflame,
yet the bush was not consumed.

15

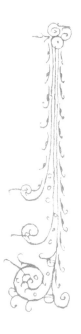

Moses said, 'I must turn aside to look at this
marvellous sight; why doesn't the bush burn up?'
When God saw that he had turned aside to look, God called him out
of the bush: 'Moses! Moses!' He answered, 'Here I am.'
And God continued, 'Now the cry of the Israelites has reached me;
moreover, I have seen how the Egyptians oppress them.
Come, therefore, I will send you to Pharaoh, and you shall free my
people, the Israelites, from Egypt.'
But Moses said to God, 'Who am I that I should go to Pharaoh and
free the Israelites from Egypt?'
And God said, 'I will be with you; that shall be your sign that it was
I who sent you. And when you have freed the people from Egypt,
you shall worship God at this mountain.'

(EXODUS 3:1–4, 9–12)

CREDENTIALS FOR LEADERSHIP

Once, when Moses was keeping Jethro's flock in the wilderness, a
little kid escaped from him. When it reached a shady place, a pool of
water appeared before it and it stopped to drink. When Moses caught
up with it, he said, 'I did not know that you ran away because you
were thirsty, you must be weary.' So he put the kid on his shoulder
and carried it back. Then God said: 'Because you have shown
compassion to the flock of a human owner, you shall most surely
lead my flock, the people of Israel.'

(MIDRASH EXODUS RABBAH 2:2)

TEN LIFE PRINCIPLES

God spoke all these words saying:

*I, the Eternal am your God who brought you out of the land of
Egypt, the house of bondage:*

You shall have no other gods beside me.

*You shall not make for yourself a sculptured image or any likeness
of what is in the heavens above or on the earth below or
in the waters under the earth. You shall not bow down
to them or serve them.*

*You shall not swear falsely by the name of the Eternal your God for
God will not clear one who swears falsely by God's name.*

*Remember the Sabbath day and keep it holy. Six days you shall
labour and do all your work, but the seventh day is a Sabbath
of the Eternal your God.*

*Honour your father and your mother that you may long endure on
the land that the Eternal your God is giving you.*

You shall not murder.

You shall not commit adultery.

You shall not steal.

You shall not bear false witness against your neighbour.

You shall not covet anything that is your neighbour's.

(EXODUS 20:1–14, ABRIDGED)

GOD'S LAW

And now O Israel, what does the Eternal your God demand of you?

*Only this, to revere the Eternal your God, to walk only in God's
paths, to love God and to serve the Eternal your God with all
your heart and soul,*

Keeping God's commandments and laws which I enjoin upon you
today for your good.
For the Eternal God is God supreme, the great, the mighty and the
awesome God who shows no favour and takes no bribe,
But upholds the cause of the orphan and the widow and befriends the
stranger providing him with food and clothing. You too must
befriend the stranger, for you were strangers in the land of Egypt.

(DEUTERONOMY 10:12–13, 17–19)

MIRIAM
JOYOUS SPIRIT
THIRTEENTH CENTURY BCE, SINAI

Then Miriam, the prophetess, Aaron's sister,
took a timbrel in her hand, and all the women
went out after her in dance with timbrels.
And Miriam chanted for them: Sing to the Eternal One,
for God has triumphed gloriously.

(EXODUS 15:20–1)

The prophetess Miriam was the elder sister of Moses and Aaron and, alongside her two younger brothers, she played a significant part in the liberation of the Israelites from Egypt. Her role was particular and distinctive: whereas Moses was the people's legislator, and Aaron was given the part of priest, Miriam was the Israelites' spiritual leader, nurturing them with her positive spirit and faith as they journeyed through the desert in search of the Promised Land of Canaan. As described in Exodus 15, after leading the people across the Red Sea with her brothers, she was moved to take up a timbrel (a kind of hand drum or tambourine) and, praising God, led the women in a choral dance of victory. She realized the importance of marking their arrival on the shores with such celebration. By responding to God's presence on their journey with an act of joyful praise, she was acknowledging that the miraculous nature of their crossing would stand for all time as a symbol of God's act of redemption. Significantly, it is at this moment that the Bible grants her the title 'prophetess'.

According to rabbinic tradition, Miriam is considered a prophetess in part also because of her ability to see the future, and to take action to ensure that these visions came to pass. The rabbinic stories (Midrashim) reflect on her understanding of Moses' ultimate importance even at his birth. Her name is not

given in these earlier chapters of Exodus, but it was undoubtedly Miriam who watched over her baby brother when – fearful of Pharaoh's edict that all Hebrew male infants be killed – their mother, Amram, hid him in the reeds of the Nile. When Pharaoh's daughter came across the baby while bathing, it was Miriam who had the ingenious idea of advising her to use Moses' mother as a nurse for him.

After serving the children of Israel for many years, Miriam eventually died in the wilderness and was buried there. According to rabbinic tradition, a miraculous well of water that had accompanied the Israelites on their wanderings dried up after her death, but it reappeared shortly afterwards, moving with the Israelites, and providing for them throughout the rest of their journey. Jewish tradition teaches that just as Miriam had sustained her people with her vision and joyous spirit in life, so her well of water continued after her death to give life and hope to her brothers and to the people she had protected and served.

TRUSTING IN THE FUTURE

Where could the Israelites have got timbrels and flutes in the wilderness? It was simply that the faithful ones had been confident and knew that God would do miracles and mighty deeds for them at their going out of Egypt, so they prepared for themselves timbrels and flutes. And Miriam sang to them. Just as Moses recited the song for the men, so Miriam recited the song for the women.

(MEKHILTA SHIRATA 10)

SEEING THE FUTURE

Miriam prophesied, 'My mother is destined to give birth to a son who will save Israel'; and when the house was flooded with light at the birth of Moses, her father arose and kissed her head and said: 'My daughter, your prophecy has been fulfilled.' Thus she is called Miriam, the prophetess (Exodus 15:20). But later, when she was

casting him into the river, her mother struck her on the head, saying: 'My daughter, what about your prophecy now?' This is why the Bible says that she stood near the Nile, in order to see what would become of her prophecy.

(EXODUS RABBAH 1:22)

SUSTAINING THE PEOPLE

The well of water that followed the people in the desert was because of the merit of Miriam. Just after Miriam's death, the people complained that there was no water and God provided a well of water. How was it constructed? It was rock-shaped like a kind of beehive and wherever they journeyed it rolled along and came with them. When the standard bearers halted and the tabernacle was set up, that same rock would come and settle down in the court of the tent of meeting and the elders would come and stand upon it and say, 'Spring up, O well,' and water would flow.

(NUMBERS RABBAH 1:2)

SAMUEL
MORAL LEADER
ELEVENTH CENTURY BCE, ISRAEL

Young Samuel was in the service of God under Eli.
In those days the word of God was rare;
prophecy was not widespread.

(1 SAMUEL 3:1)

Samuel lived more than two hundred years after Moses had brought the Ten Commandments from Mount Sinai, at a time when the original vision of the Israelites as a special people with a holy purpose had faded into obscurity. He was born to Hannah, a previously barren woman who repaid God's gift of fertility by devoting Samuel's life to service in the Jerusalem Temple. But the house of high priest Eli was far from the holy place Hannah envisaged: the priest's sons were unworthy of their father and exploited their roles as priests. The book of Samuel relates that one night while Samuel and Eli were both asleep, God called out to Samuel, but – in an allegory of the society around him – the boy does not recognize God's call, thinking instead that Eli is calling him. God calls three times and Samuel wakes Eli three times before the aged high priest realizes that this is a divine message intended for a new prophet in Israel: the young boy, Samuel.

With this first difficult message, in which God warned of the fall of the house of Eli, Samuel began his lifelong career as a prophet and judge. He developed from a *ro'eh* (a prophet who predicts the future) into a *navi* (one who also communicates the will of God), as he made the rounds of Israel's tribal territories,

Bethel, Gilgal and Mizpah, and brought insight and justice to the people. His central contribution to the prophetic role in Israelite society was his absolute insistence on morality in leadership. As a leader himself, Samuel fervently believed that all those in positions of power – whether kings, priests or tribal chiefs – were in the service of God and the people, not themselves. He taught that only a blameless and moral person, a servant of God, is capable of being a good leader in society, and this issue remains topical today.

In Samuel's old age, the tribes of Israel found themselves threatened by a Philistine invasion, and the people called out for unity against the enemy. Samuel resisted the call for the establishment of a monarchy, warning of the dangers that investing one person with absolute control would bring to the moral life of the nation. The troubled Israelites rejected their prophet's warnings, however, and so Samuel reluctantly appointed Saul as king. Saul tragically proceeded to demonstrate the weaknesses that Samuel had foretold, and eventually died in battle. Samuel had already anointed David in his place, but he continued to act as a prophet, holding King David to Israel's Covenant with God.

ETHICAL LEADERSHIP

'I have been your leader from my youth to this day.
Here I am! Testify against me, in the presence of God and in the
*   presence of God's anointed king. Whose ox have I taken,*
*   or whose ass have I taken?*
Whom have I defrauded or whom have I robbed? From whom have I
*   taken a bribe to look the other way? I will return it you.'*
They responded, 'You have not defrauded us, and you have not
*   robbed us and you have not taken anything from anyone.'*

(I Samuel 12:2–4)

GOD'S REQUIREMENTS

Samuel said:

> *'Does God delight in burnt offerings and sacrifices*
> *as much as in obedience to the Eternal One's command?*
> *Surely obedience is better than sacrifice,*
> *compliance than the fat of rams.*
> *For rebellion is like the sin of divination,*
> *defiance like the iniquity of idols.'*

(I SAMUEL 15:22–3)

THE POTENTIAL CORRUPTION OF MONARCHY

Samuel reported all the words of God to the people,
> *who were asking him for a king.*
He said, 'This will be the practice of the king who will rule over you.
He will take your sons and appoint them as his charioteers and
> *horsemen, and they will be as out-runners for his chariots.*
He will appoint them as his chiefs of thousands and of fifties; or they
> *will have to plough his fields, reap his harvest, and make his*
> *weapons and the equipment for his chariots.*
He will take your daughters as perfumers, cooks and bakers.
He will seize your choice fields, vineyards and olive groves,
> *and give them to his courtiers.*
The day will come when you cry out because of the king
> *whom you yourselves have chosen; and God will not*
> *answer you on that day.'*

(I SAMUEL 8:10–14, 18)

AMOS
FEARLESS CRITIC
EIGHTH CENTURY BCE, ISRAEL

I have wrought destruction among you
As when God destroyed Sodom and Gomorrah;
You have become like a brand plucked from burning.
Yet you have not turned back to me, declares God.
Assuredly, because you are acting thus towards me,
Even so will I act towards you, O Israel –
Prepare to meet your God, O Israel!

(AMOS 4:11–12)

The prophet Amos rose from humble beginnings, as a shepherd and cultivator of sycamore trees in rural Judah, to become a critic of those in power and of the entire civilization of the Near East. More than any of the other biblical prophets, he was fearless in his verbal attacks on injustice and the self-satisfaction of the rich and powerful of his day. Armed with God's word, he travelled north from his farmlands to the kingdom of Israel as a young man to preach God's message in the streets of Bethel. It was in this town not far from Jerusalem, where the slave trade flourished and even children were sold for profit, that he realized how far the people had sunk into corruption and deviated from moral law. The iniquity on the streets was only reinforced by the immorality demonstrated on the national level, as the kingdoms surrounding Israel vied for supremacy and struggled to accumulate wealth and territory. Amos's list of the transgressions of humanity – slavery, poverty, injustice, war and oppression – marks the beginning of a continuous written record of ill treatment of one people towards another.

Amos believed that because God had chosen Israel for a special task, Israel would be the first to suffer for her sins. He used the image of a plumb line in his speeches to indicate that God would measure the Israelites according to how far they strayed from the straight path. He attacked the luxurious living of the rich – their elegant palaces, pleasant vineyards and addiction to wine – and pointed to the exploitation of the poor that this opulence relied upon. He saw how religious observance, overseen by a corrupt priesthood, had become entrenched in ritual rather than piety, and concluded that the Israelites – who as God's chosen people should know better – had lost all sense of moral values. When Amos finally condemned Israel to exile and its king to banishment (Amos 7:11), the people's indignation became active protest, and Amaziah, the priest of Bethel, sent word to King Jeroboam that a maverick prophet was preaching treason. Amos was relentless in his criticism, however, and predicted that Amaziah himself would be doomed if he too did not live up to his responsibilities as a representative of God's law. Like his contemporary, Hosea, Amos foresaw that without the protective shield of moral law and a just society, the Israelites would be unable to weather the storms of warring empires. His teachings have given the world an ethical standard to which all people can aspire.

PRINCIPLES OF RELIGION
Seek good and not evil,
 that you may live,
 and that the Eternal God
 may truly be with you
 as you think.
Hate evil and love good,
 and establish justice in the gate.
I loathe, I spurn your festivals,
 I am not appeased by your solemn assemblies.
If you offer me burnt offerings – or your meal offerings –
 I will not accept them;

I will pay no heed to your gifts of fatlings.
Spare me the sound of your hymns.
   Let me not hear the music of your lutes.
But let justice well up like water,
   righteousness, like an unfailing stream.

(Amos 5:14–15, 21–4)

A PEOPLE WITH A SPECIAL TASK

Hear this word, O people of Israel,
   that God has spoken concerning you,
   concerning the whole family that I brought up
   from the land of Egypt:
You alone have I singled out
   of all the families of the earth –
   that is why I will call you to account
   for all your iniquities.

(Amos 3:1–2)

HOSEA
LOVING REBUKER
EIGHTH CENTURY BCE, ISRAEL

Return, O Israel, to the Eternal your God,
For you have fallen because of your sin.

(HOSEA 14:2)

The relationship of the people of Israel with God is often said to be like a marriage. Hosea, whose prophetic career spanned the last years of King Jeroboam II's reign and the period of anarchy that followed, witnessed the Israelite nation straying from this marriage, breaking its Covenant with God and worshipping instead the local gods of the land. Meanwhile, as notions of justice and caring were abandoned and society became steadily more corrupt, the powerful Assyrian empire stood by, plotting to conquer a weakened nation.

Just as Israel was a faithless nation to God, so was the woman Hosea loved and married unfaithful to him. Gomer, like Israel, entered into a marriage but then ignored all her responsibilities, eventually abandoning her home, family and her children. Yet Hosea was unswerving hin his love for Gomer throughout, choosing to forgive her for her loose ways and the other men in her life. He even named Gomer's children Lo-ruhamah, meaning 'not pitied', and Lo-ammmi, 'not my people', in acknowledgement that they were not his. When Gomer decided to leave Hosea for another man, Hosea's love and forgiveness continued nonetheless, without condition. Hosea's personal story became his prophetic message, as he used his own experience of his relationship with his wayward wife to preach to the people the message of loyalty and trust that a true marriage requires. Many passages in the book of Hosea therefore have a double meaning, referring to both 'marriages' at once. His description of God's betrothal with Israel (Hosea 2:19–20)

is used today in the daily binding of *tefillin* (the prayer boxes worn during prayers) and sometimes in the Jewish wedding ceremony.

When everyone else had rejected Gomer, Hosea took her back, but first made her sit alone for many days. So, Hosea prophesied, would Israel sit solitary without rulers or land if she continued to practise Godless ways. He preached God's love and forgiveness for the people even though they strayed from the Commandments. He also taught that eventually such behaviour undermines the very nature of the relationship. Through the metaphor of a marriage, he offered the people a chance to turn from the path of self-destruction that loomed before them: his call for repentance (Hosea 14:2) is read each year on *Shabbat Shuvah* ('Shabbat of Returning') prior to Yom Kippur. Hosea's warnings ultimately went unheeded – and in 721 BCE the Northern Kingdom fell to Assyria – but his gentle words continue to inspire us today with their message of the constancy of God's love.

GOD'S BETROTHAL TO THE PEOPLE

I will betroth you to me for ever.
I will betroth you to me with righteousness and justice,
And with goodness and mercy.
I will betroth you to me with faithfulness.
Then you shall be devoted to God.

(HOSEA 2:19–20)

DESTRUCTION OF LAND AND PEOPLE

Hear the word of God, O people of Israel.
For God has a case against the inhabitants of this land,
Because there is no honesty and no goodness
And no obedience to God in the land.
False swearing, dishonesty and murder
And theft and adultery are rife.

Crime follows crime.
For that, the earth is withered.
Everything that dwells on it languishes –
Beasts of the field and birds of the sky –
Even the fish of the sea perish.

(HOSEA 4:1–3)

CALL FOR REPENTANCE

Come, let us turn back to God.
God attacked, and God can heal us.
God wounded, and God can bind us up.
In two days God will make us whole again;
On the third day God will raise us up;
And we shall be whole by God's favour.
Let us pursue obedience to the Eternal One,
And we shall become obedient.
God's appearance is as sure as daybreak.
And God will come to us like rain,
Like latter rain that refreshes the earth.

(HOSEA 6:1–3)

GOD'S ETERNAL PROMISE OF LOVE

I will be to Israel like dew.
They shall blossom like the lily,
They shall strike root like a tree in Lebanon.
Their boughs shall spread out far,
Their beauty shall be like the olive tree's,
Their fragrance like that of Lebanon.

(HOSEA 14:5–9)

ISAIAH
VISIONARY OF PEACE
EIGHTH CENTURY BCE, JUDAH

Seek justice;
Relieve the oppressed,
Defend the orphan,
Plead for the widow.

(ISAIAH 1:17)

Isaiah's dramatic call to prophecy, narrated in the first person in Isaiah 6, can be dated at around 742 BCE, the year of King Uzziah of Judah's death. The prophet recalls how as a young man, while meditating in the Temple court, he experienced an awesome vision of God seated on a high throne, filling the Temple with radiance and majesty. Overwhelmed by such contact with the Divine, Isaiah was at first moved to declare his unworthiness, but became agonizingly aware that it was to be his onerous task to take God's message to the people of Judah and the city of Jerusalem. The first thirty-nine chapters of Isaiah are a forceful record of his prophetic mission. (The remaining twenty-seven chapters, known as 2nd Isaiah or Deutero-Isaiah, were written long after his death.)

Judah in Isaiah's time was continually threatened with the westward expansion of the power-hungry Assyrian Empire, and when the Northern Kingdom fell to the Assyrian army in 721 BCE, many Judeans couldn't help but feel they were about to receive similar punishment for their own erring ways. In a desperate effort to retain Judah's independence, the rulers of the Southern Kingdom sought makeshift alliances with the aggressor, a strategy that Isaiah despised. With unshakeable belief and faith, the prophet urged reliance on God alone. It seemed that his words had been miraculously vindicated when in 701 BCE, the King of Assyria stood with his army at the walls of Jerusalem, but was forced by a sudden and inexplicable plague to depart without a fight.

The prophet's strongest invective was reserved for his own people. He was painfully aware of the sinfulness of the nation, one 'laden with iniquity and offspring of evil' (Isaiah 1:4), and of the self-destructiveness of its immoral course. Even his beloved Jerusalem – for Isaiah the centre of the spiritual world and the symbol for his vision of the future – came under attack: 'See how the faithful city has become a harlot that was once full of justice' (Isaiah 1:21).

Isaiah is probably the best known of the biblical prophets. His fiery oratory and vision have fired the imagination of Jewish and non-Jewish thinkers and activists to this day. Despite his frequent warnings of destruction and disaster, he also believed that the catastrophic tide could be reversed with a change in people's behaviour, and he held out a messianic hope for the survival of a remnant of the people at the culmination of history. His vision of peace (Isaiah 2:4) is carved into the wall facing the United Nations building in New York – emphasizing the world's hope for a universal kinship for which we all must continue to work and wait.

LEARN TO DO GOOD

What need have I of all your sacrifices, says God.
And when you lift up your hands,
I will turn my eyes away from you.
Though you pray at length,
I will not listen.
Your hands are stained with crime –
Wash yourselves clean.
Put your evil doings away from my sight.
Cease to do evil.
Learn to do good.
(ISAIAH 1:11, 15–16)

SURVIVAL OF A REMNANT

Then I heard the voice of God saying,
'Whom shall I send? Who will go for us?'
And I said, 'Here am I; send me.'
And God said, 'Go say to that people.
Hear, indeed, but do not understand;
See, indeed, but do not grasp.'
Dull that people's mind,
Stop its ears, and seal its eyes –
Lest, seeing with its eyes
And hearing with its ears,
It also grasp with its mind,
And repent and save itself.'
I asked, 'How long, God?' and God replied:
'Till towns lie waste without inhabitants
And houses without people,
And the ground lies waste and desolate –
For the Lord will banish the population –
And deserted sites are many
In the midst of the land.
But while a tenth part yet remains in it, it shall repent.
It shall be ravaged like the terbinth and the oak,
Of which stumps are left even when they are felled:
Its stump shall be a holy seed.'
(Isaiah 6:8–13)

LIGHT OF REDEMPTION

The people that walked in darkness
Have seen a brilliant light;

On those who dwelt in a land of gloom
Light has dawned.
You have magnified that nation,
Have given it great joy;
They have rejoiced before You
As they rejoice at reaping time,
As they exult when dividing spoil.

(ISAIAH 9:2–3)

FUTURE VISION FOR JERUSALEM

In the days to come,
The mountain of God's house
Shall stand firm above the mountains
And tower above the hills;
And all the nations shall gaze on it with joy.
And the many peoples shall go and say:
'Come, let us go up to the mountain of God,
To the house of the God of Jacob;
That God may instruct us in God's ways,
And that we may walk in God's paths.'
For instruction shall come forth from Zion,
The word of God from Jerusalem.
Thus God will judge among the nations
And arbitrate for many peoples.
And they shall beat their swords into ploughshares,
And their spears into pruning hooks.
Nation shall not take up sword against nation.
They shall never again know war.

(ISAIAH 2:2–4)

FUTURE VISION FOR THE WORLD
The wolf will dwell with the lamb,
The leopard lie down with the kid;
The calf, the young lion and the fatling together,
With a little boy to herd them.
The cow and the bear shall graze,
Their young shall lie down together;
And the lion like the ox shall eat straw.
A babe shall play
Over a viper's hole,
And an infant pass his hand
Over an adder's den.
In all of my sacred mountain,
Nothing evil or vile shall be done.
For the earth shall be full of the knowledge of God
As the waters cover the seas.

(ISAIAH 11:6–9)

MICAH
CHAMPION OF THE LOWLY
EIGHTH CENTURY BCE, JUDAH

I am filled with strength by the spirit of God,
And with judgement and courage,
To declare to Jacob his transgressions
And to Israel his sin.

(MICAH 3:8)

Micah lived in the last part of the eighth century BCE, just before the final collapse of the Northern Kingdom of Israel. Born in the small village of Moresheth-Gath in the foothills of the Judean mountains, he moved to Jerusalem, the capital of Judah, but the spiritual and symbolic centre of both kingdoms. Micah emerged as a voice of the people at a time of economic hardship, political intrigue and religious hypocrisy. His prophetic messages, uttered with powerful clarity, are devastating attacks on the injustices of society. Prophesying that God would not allow such injustices to continue, he foretold disaster for the whole nation.

Micah identified with the ordinary people, the farmers who grew olives and raised cattle. He spoke out passionately against the misery and degradation he saw all around him, and he chastised the ruling classes for their exploitation of the poor, calling the suffering they imposed a sin against God's design for a holy nation. He condemned the rich landowners who dispossessed those who could not pay their exorbitant rents, and he criticized abuses of power by the judges, the prevalence of bribery and the decay of natural justice. Micah also attacked the priests, who favoured the rich and made no attempt to alleviate the sufferings of the poor. For these priests, the centre of religious life was the offering of sacrifices and Micah spoke out against those who devoted themselves to punctilious

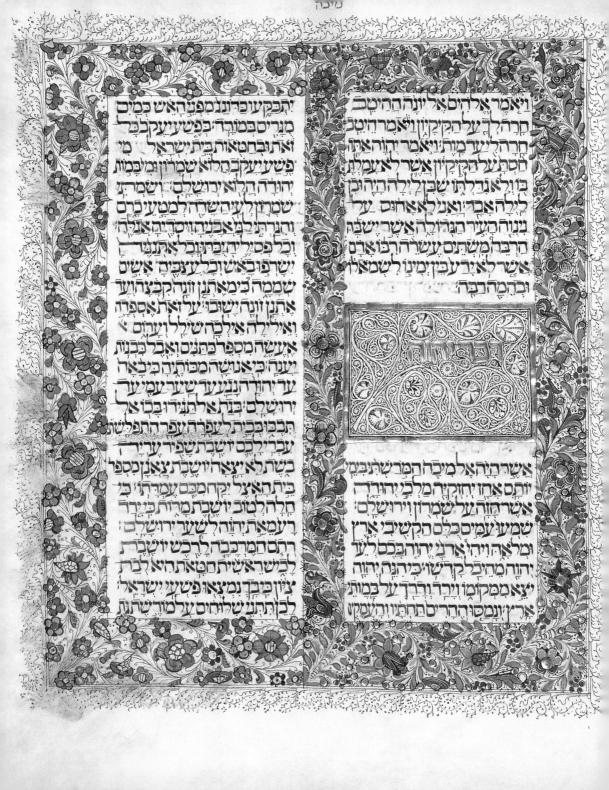

ויאמר אלהים אל יונה ההיטב
חרה לך על הקיקיון ויאמר היטב
חרה לי עד מות ויאמר יהוה אתה
חסת על הקיקיון אשר לא עמלת
בו ולא גדלתו שבן לילה היה ובן
לילה אבד ואני לא אחוס על
נינוה העיר הגדולה אשר ישבה
הרבה משתים עשרה רבו אדם
אשר לא ידע בין ימינו לשמאלו
ובהמה רבה

דבר יהוה

אשר היה אל מיכה המרשתי בימי
יותם אחז יחזקיה מלכי יהודה
אשר חזה על שמרון וירושלם
שמעו עמים כלם הקשיבי ארץ
ומלאה ויהי אדני יהוה בכם לעד
יהוה מהיכל קדשו כי הנה יהוה
יצא ממקומו וירד ודרך על במותי
ארץ ונמסו ההרים תחתיו והעמקים

יתבקעו כדונג מפני האש כמים
מגרים במורד בפשע יעקב כל
זאת ובחטאות בית ישראל מי
פשע יעקב הלוא שמרון ומי במות
יהודה הלוא ירושלם ושמתי
שמרון לעי השדה למטעי כרם
והגרתי לגי אבניה וסדיה אגלה
וכל פסיליה יכתו וכל אתנניה
ישרפו באש וכל עצביה אשים
שממה כי מאתנן זונה קבצה ועד
אתנן זונה ישובו על זאת אספדה
ואילילה אילכה שילל וערום
אעשה מספד כתנים ואבל כבנות
יענה כי אנושה מכותיה כי באה
עד יהודה נגע עד שער עמי עד
ירושלם כבת אל תגידי בגת בכו
בבו כבית לעפרה עפר התפלשתי
עברי לכם יושבת שפיר עריה
בשת לא יצאה יושבת צאנן מספד
בית האצל יקח מכם עמדתו כי
חלה לטוב יושבת מרות כי ירד
רע מאת יהוה לשער ירושלם
רתם המרכבה לרכש יושבת
לכיש ראשית חטאת היא לבת
ציון כי בך נמצאו פשעי ישראל
לכן תתני שלוחים על מורשת

religious observance in this way and yet led immoral lives and were blind to the moral abuses around them. For Micah, the evils of society comprised heartless abuse of the weak by the strong and a failure of false prophets to grasp the true meaning of religion. Yet, even though the people misunderstood the nature of an ethical religious life, Micah still held on to the hope of a just and righteous nation.

As Micah and his contemporaries rightly foresaw, a time of destruction was to come. In 721 BCE, the Assyrian Empire conquered Israel and exiled its inhabitants, repopulating the land with exiles from other defeated states. The Ten Lost Tribes of Israel and their whereabouts became shrouded in myth and the potential for a Jewish state to be a 'light to the nations' was lost.

Although Micah's fundamental aim was to undo the wrongs of social injustice, he also brought comfort to his people. Micah predicted the restoration of Israel in the form of a more virtuous nation. His vision remains true today in the Jewish belief in a universal framework of justice and compassion.

A WARNING TO THE PEOPLE

Listen, all you peoples,
Give heed O Earth, and all it holds;
And let me Eternal God be your accuser –
My God from God's holy abode.
For lo! The Eternal
Is coming forth from God's dwelling place,
God will come down and stride
Upon the heights of the earth.
The mountains shall melt under God
And the valleys burst open –
Like wax before fire,
Like water cascading down a slope.

(MICAH 1:2–4)

THE EXPLOITATION OF THE POOR

Ah, those who plan iniquity
And design evil in their beds;
When morning dawns, they do it,
For they have the power.
They covet fields, and seize them;
Houses, and take them away.
They defraud men of their homes,
And people of their land.
You arise as an enemy to my people.
You strip the mantle
Off peaceful folk passing by
Whose thoughts are far from conflict.
You drive the women of my people away
From their pleasant homes;
And condemn their children
To hopeless slavery.
Get up and get out!
You are trespassing here.
The land is defiled
And for this it is doomed
To irrevocable disaster.
(MICAH 2:1–2, 8–10)

A VISION OF THE FUTURE

In the days to come,
The Mount of God's House shall stand
Firm above the mountains;

And it shall tower over the hills.
The people shall gaze on it with joy.
And the many nations shall go and say:
Come, let us go up
To the Mount of the Eternal One,
To the House of the God of Jacob;
That God may instruct us in God's ways,
And that we may walk in God's paths.

(MICAH 4:1–2)

RIGHT RELIGION

With what shall I approach God,
Do homage to God on High?
Shall I approach God with burnt offerings,
With calves of a year old?
Will God be pleased with thousands of rams,
With myriads of streams of oil?
Shall I give my first born for my transgression,
The fruit of my body for sins?
God has told you, O mortals, what is good,
And what God requires of you:
Only to do justice
And to love goodness,
And to walk humbly with God.

(MICAH 6:6–8)

JEREMIAH
HERALD OF DOOM, BRINGER OF HOPE
SIXTH CENTURY BCE, JUDAH

Restrain your voice from weeping,
Your eyes from shedding tears.
There is hope for your future, declares God.
Your children shall return to their place.

(JEREMIAH 31:16–17)

In English, a Jeremiah is someone who habitually prophesies disaster, and 'herald of doom' is certainly a valid description of this apparently merciless prophet. Although Jeremiah initially protested against his calling, pleading youth and shyness as Isaiah and Moses had before him, the Bible relates that once he had accepted his role, he was relentless in his attacks on the faithlessness of the people and the society he saw straying so far from Moses' law. His searing message of destruction foretold the end of the Israelite nation, the exile of the people and the desolation of Jerusalem. In one of his most vitriolic speeches, delivered against false prophets, the word of God was said to burst from his lips 'like fire and like a hammer that breaks rock to pieces' (Jeremiah 23:29). Standing in the very place where the priests performed the ceremonies of the sacrificial cult, Jeremiah dared to denounce the people's reliance on ritual sacrifice and their worship of heathen gods, just as Micah had done a hundred years before. His angry condemnations, borne out of the intense pain his prophecy caused him, provoked a near riot. He was subsequently placed on trial for treason and sedition.

Jeremiah was eventually released but he would not stay silent. It was his agonizing and thankless task to warn of the terrible events to come, thereby remaining alienated from the society in which he lived. When his prophecies concerning the destruction of the monarchy and the Temple were read out to the new King Jehoiakim of Judah, the king burned the scroll and ordered his rearrest. In 586 BCE, this same king witnessed Jerusalem's fall to the Babylonians and the people's exile in captivity to Babylon.

For all Jeremiah's foretelling of doom, he is also remembered for his message of comfort and hope. Realizing that the exiles would become the saving remnant of the people, he wrote urging them to settle and prosper in Babylon and, to demonstrate his faith in the ultimate future, purchased a plot of land in Anathoth, the village of his birth. He advised the people that they could be Jews even if they did not live in their own land, and he laid down a principle that has remained with the Jewish people from that time until now: that when in exile, they should seek the peace of the country in which they live. His message continued to offer hope to the people of their eventual return to their land, although he himself died in exile in Egypt.

MEND YOUR WAYS

Thus says the God of Israel: Mend your ways and your actions and
*   I will let you dwell in this place.*
Do not put your trust in illusions and say:
*   This is the Temple of the*
*   Eternal One . . . No, if*
*   you really mend your*
*   ways and your actions;*
*   if you execute justice*
*   between one man and*
*   another;*
If you do not oppress the
*   stranger, the orphan,*
*   and the widow;*

If you do not shed the blood
>   of the innocent in this place; if you do not follow other gods,
>   to your own hurt;
Then only will I let you dwell in this place, in the land that I gave to
>   your ancestors for all time.

(JEREMIAH 7:3–7)

BITTER WEEPING

Thus says God:
A cry is heard in Ramah,
Wailing, bitter weeping,
Rachel weeping for her children.
She refuses to be comforted
For her children who are no more.

(JEREMIAH 31:15)

CLAY IN THE HANDS OF THE POTTER

The word which came to Jeremiah from God:
Go down to the house of a potter, and there I will impart my
>   *words to you.*
So I went down to the house of a potter, and found him working
>   *at the wheel.*
And if the vessel he was making was spoiled, as happens to clay
>   *in the potter's hands, he would make it into another vessel;*
>   *such as the potter saw fit to make.*
Then the word of God came to me.
O House of Israel, can I not deal with you like this potter?
Just like clay in the hands of the potter, so are you in my hands.
At one moment I may decree that a nation or kingdom shall be

uprooted and pulled down and destroyed.
But if that nation against which I made the decree turns back
    from its wickedness, I change my mind concerning the
    punishment I planned to bring on it.

(JEREMIAH 18:1–8)

COMFORT IN EXILE

Thus says the God of Israel to the whole community,
    which I exiled from Jerusalem to Babylonia.
Build houses and live in them, plant gardens and eat their fruit.
Take wives and beget sons and daughters and take wives for your
    sons and give your daughters to husbands that they may
    bear sons and daughters.
Multiply there, do not decrease.
And seek the welfare of the city to which I have exiled you and
    pray to God on its behalf, for in its prosperity you shall prosper.

(JEREMIAH 29:4–7)

A RENEWED ISRAEL

See, a time is coming – declares the Eternal One – when I will make
    a new Covenant with the House of Israel and the House of Judah.
Such is the Covenant I will make with the house of Israel after these
    days, declares God. I will put my teaching into their innermost
    being and inscribe it upon their hearts. Then I will be their God
    and they shall be my people.
No longer will they need to teach each other and say to one another,
Heed the Eternal One; for all of them, from the least of them to
    the greatest, shall heed me – declares God.

(JEREMIAH 31:31, 33–4)

HILLEL
SAINTLY SAGE
60 BCE–10 CE, JUDEA

What is hateful to you
Do not do to your neighbour.
That is the entire Torah,
All the rest is commentary.
Go and learn it.

(Talmud Shabbat 31a)

Hillel, born in Babylon, came to Jerusalem as a young man to study with the foremost scholars of his day. Even though he had to earn a living outside his studies, his endeavours were remarkable, leading to a new understanding of the Torah. His teachings, recorded in the Mishnah – the rabbinic codification of Jewish law – promote a liberal and flexible interpretation of Moses' law that accords with the changing nature of economic and social life. He promoted the democratization of Judaism, away from the exclusive and esoteric sacrificial cult of the Temple and its dynasty of priesthood, to a life of learning for all, centred on the synagogue as a place of community, prayer and learning. As President of the Religious Court (Sanhedrin) and leader of the Pharisees, he was radical in his acceptance of a double law: the written one traditionally ascribed to Moses in the Torah, and the oral one that had developed out of the deliberations and commentaries of the rabbis. It is through this notion of oral law that Judaism is able to adapt to contemporary circumstances, even today.

In discussing prophecy, the Talmud (Sotah 48b) assigns the divine spirit to Hillel – although it also suggests that his generation was not worthy of his teachings. Hillel's prophetic status stems from his deep knowledge of Jewish law, which he combined with an overriding compassion and concern for the ordinary

person. His attachment to the people and his commitment to peace between individuals and societies stood in stark contrast to the violence and corruption of King Herod's state in which he lived, and was in keeping with the traditions of the biblical prophet in its placing of integrity and faith above nation and law in all things.

Hillel's scholarly partner and critic in the Sanhedrin was Shammai. Shammai took a more stringent line in interpreting the Torah and, when confronted by a potential convert who deliberately tried to provoke him by demanding to be taught the whole law while standing on one foot, he reacted by sending the man away in anger. Hillel, however, received the antagonist gently, with the declaration that the whole Torah concerns the love we should have for one another, and that the rest is commentary to be studied (Talmud Shabbat 31a). With these words, he gave a new direction to Judaism – a practice of loving-kindness in the spirit of the law that extends above and beyond the letter of the law. Hillel constructed a living bridge between the Torah and life, which remains in place to this day.

INDIVIDUAL RESPONSIBILITY

If I am not for myself, who is for me?
And if only for myself, what am I?
And if not now, when?

(MISHNAH AVOT 1:14)

LIVING IN COMMUNITY

Do not separate yourself from the community.
Trust not yourself until the day of death.
Judge not your fellow man
Before you have come into his situation.
Say not a thing that cannot be understood at once
In the assumption that sometime in the future

It will be understood.
Say not when I shall have leisure I shall study,
Perhaps you will not have the leisure.

(MISHNAH AVOT 2:5)

LEARNING FOR LIFE

Hillel used to say,
The more flesh the more worms,
The more possessions the more worry.
The more Torah the more life,
The more study and contemplation
*   the more wisdom,*
The more counsel the more discernment,
The more charity the more peace.
The one who acquires a good name,
*   acquires it for him or herself.*
The one who acquires knowledge of the Law,
*   acquires life in the world to come.*

(MISHNAH AVOT 2:7)

YOHANAN BEN ZAKKAI
SPIRITUAL RESISTOR
FIRST CENTURY CE, JUDEA

Rabban Yohanan ben Zakkai used to say,
If there is a plant in your hand
when they say to you:
Behold the Messiah has come!
Go plant the plant and afterwards
go out to greet him.

(AVOT DE RABBI NATHAN B, 31)

As the Roman army besieged Jerusalem in the first century and laid waste to all in its path, Rabbi Yohanan ben Zakkai realized that decisive action was necessary to ensure a future for Judaism. Yohanan was the youngest student of Hillel and the leading *tanna* (sage) of his time, with a reputation for wisdom that earned him an authority and influence far beyond his own circle. Desiring a peaceful solution to the conflict with Rome, he had urged his many followers to restrain their anger against the occupiers. However, he also recognized that the extremist Jewish groups defending Jerusalem were likely only to hasten the city's destruction. Risking both his life and his reputation, he abandoned the people and the Jerusalem Temple (rebuilt following the return of the exiles from Babylon) by faking his own death and arranging to be carried out of the city for burial through Jewish and Roman lines.

Once outside the city walls, Yohanan made his way to Vespasian, the Roman general who was leading the attack, and greeted him with an unexpected, 'Hail, Emperor'. Flattered by the rabbi's prophecy of his future status, Vespasian granted Yohanan's request to start a small academy at the coastal town of Yavneh, where Jewish religious life and learning could continue. As Yohanan had foreseen, Emperor Nero died shortly afterwards and Vespasian was called back to Rome to be proclaimed emperor in 69 CE. When Jerusalem was burned by the Romans in 70 CE and the people were exiled, Yohanan's academy kept the light of Jewish religious life and learning alive, ensuring that its intellectual traditions and its spiritual essence would live on.

As a prophet of Israel, Yohanan preached that God's Covenant transcended time and place. The destruction of the Second Temple had a profound effect on the remnant of the people, seeming to symbolize the removal of God's presence from the nation. Yohanan, like Jeremiah before him, provided spiritual guidance to those left distraught and bewildered by this enormous tragedy in Jewish history. He called for a new way to live out the Jewish mission without political nationhood, without temple sacrifice or priesthood, without even Jerusalem itself. This new philosophy had its beginnings in his school at Yavneh. It was from this small academy that the rabbinic scholars of the Mishnah and Talmud were soon to emerge as the fundamental builders of the next two thousand years of Jewish law and religious life.

REBUILDING JEWISH RELIGIOUS LIFE

Once when Rabbi Yohanan ben Zakkai was leaving
Jerusalem, Rabbi Joshua was walking behind him and saw
the Temple in ruins. Rabbi Joshua said, 'Woe is us that this has been
destroyed, the place where atonement was made for the sins of
Israel.' 'No, my son, do you not know that we have a means of
making atonement that is like it. And what is it? It is deeds of love,
as it is said, 'For I desire loving kindness and not sacrifices'
(Hosea 6:6).

(Avot de Rabbi Nathan 4:21)

THE PEACEMAKER

Rabbi Yohanan ben Zakkai said, 'The stones for the building of the altar do not see nor hear nor speak, yet because they will be used to establish peace between Israel and Israel's parent in heaven, God said, "You should not wield an iron tool upon them" (Deuteronomy 27:5). How much the more then should the one who establishes peace between people, between husband and wife, between city and city, between nation and nation, between race and race, between government and government, be protected so that no harm should come to him or her.'

(Mekilta Bahodesh II)

A GOOD HEART

Rabbi Yohanan ben Zakkai said to his students, 'Go and discover what best helps one find the right way in life.' Rabbi Eliezer answered: a good eye. Rabbi Joshua answered: a good friend. Rabbi Jose answered: a good neighbour. Rabbi Simon answered: foresightedness. Rabbi Elazar answered: a good heart. Rabbi Yohanan then said to them: I prefer Rabbi Elazar's answer for his words include all of yours.

(Mishnah Avot 2:9)

AKIVA
SCHOLAR AND MARTYR
50–135 CE, JUDEA

You shall love your neighbour as yourself.
Rabbi Akiva says:
This is the greatest principle of the Torah.

(MIDRASH SIFRA 89B)

The great teacher Akiva ben Joseph, like Amos hundreds of years before him, spent the early part of his life in rural obscurity, as a shepherd in the Judean mountains. Marked by God later in life, he emerged from this simple existence with a passion for learning and teaching, and eventually entered the academy at Yavneh, established by Yohanan ben Zakkai to train a new generation of rabbinic teachers. Here he studied the intricate and complex development of the oral law, as scholars sought to expound the Torah and create a Jewish religious practice for a new era following the destruction of the Second Temple by the Roman authorities in 70 CE.

Akiva came to believe that the study of the Torah was central to Judaism. Rather than using sacrifice as a means to worship, he taught that it was possible to come close to God through studying God's law. He believed that knowledge of the Torah and the prophetic writings would lead to the fulfilment of Judaism's core purpose – that of creating a more moral, peaceful world – and his theories became a central debating point among the rabbis as they argued whether action or study was more significant. Akiva sided with study as he believed it led ultimately to

action. In demonstration of this, he translated the high ideals of the prophets into concrete statutes to sanctify the everyday lives of the people. His legislative principles included civil laws that were used to protect the rights of women, the status of the underprivileged, and the rights of free labour.

But the peace-loving values of this remarkable scholar were to be severely challenged. During the years of Roman occupation in Judea, Jewish life became steadily more restricted as persecution and oppression intensified. Akiva began by preaching obedience to Rome, believing a civilized empire would eventually tolerate and appreciate the wisdom and nature of the Jewish religion. Like the biblical prophets Jeremiah and Micah, he advocated a spiritual rather than a physical resistance to foreign influences. As each Roman edict prohibited yet more Jewish practice, Akiva was willing to submit for the sake of peace. However, when the prohibitions were extended to teaching the Torah, he refused to comply, believing it to be Judaism's essential purpose. He continued to teach despite the danger, as is remembered in a famous passage in the Passover haggadah, when five rabbis come together in secret one night to hold a Seder (the likelihood is that the rabbis were part of a revolt against Rome). For Akiva's rebellion against the Roman authorities, he was tortured and died a martyr's death, reciting as he expired, 'You shall love the Eternal your God with all your heart, with all your soul, and with all your might' (Deuteronomy 6:5), the *Sh'ma*, now the central statement of Jewish faith.

THE WATERS OF LIFE

Once the Roman government decreed that Israel should no longer occupy itself with the study of Torah. Then came Pappos ben Judah who found Rabbi Akiva studying Torah in great assemblies. He said to him, 'Akiva, are you not afraid of the Roman government?' Akiva replied with a parable, 'It is like a fox that urged the fish to come up on to dry land in order to escape the fishermen's nets. The fish answered, if we are afraid in the element in which we live, how much more should we be afraid when we are out of that element. We should then surely die. So it is with us with regard to the study of Torah which is our "life and the length of our days".'

(Talmud Berachot 6lb)

MARTYRDOM

While Akiva was being tortured, the hour for saying the Sh'ma [Deuteronomy 6] arrived. He recited it and smiled. The Roman officer called out, 'Old man, are you a sorcerer that you smile in the midst of such pain?' Akiva replied, 'All my life, I have loved God with all my heart and might and now I can truly fulfil the commandment in this prayer by loving God with all my life.' As he spoke, his soul departed.

(Talmud Berachot IX, Section 7, Fl4b)

FROM GENERATION TO GENERATION

In medieval and early modern times, Jewish philosophers and scholars were keen to apply new secular learning to establish a society based on both moral law and principles of justice and democratic ideals. Individuals such as Solomon ibn Gabirol, Bachya ibn Pakuda, Moses Maimonides and Barukh Spinoza sought through intellectual argument to demonstrate God's presence in the world as a source of ultimate good and ethical faith. Violent opposition pursued them even after their deaths, but their writings have been vindicated as truly prophetic.

Other medieval prophets carried out their role as charismatics and offered religious and spiritual guidance, drawing upon the healing powers granted to them. The Baal Shem Tov and the Hasidic *rebbe* Hannah Werbermacher inspired men and women alike to be pious adherents to a higher cause. As always, prophets also concerned themselves with the world of politics. Don Isaac Abravanel, Dona Gracia Mendes and Manasseh ben Israel fought for active justice in the face of physical oppression and, akin to the biblical prophets, challenged kings and governments in order to fulfil the destiny of the Jewish people.

These philosophers, charismatics, and statesmen and women were true descendants of the biblical prophets. They ensured that a prophetic Judaism would be enduring and vital for all generations to come.

For the earth shall be full of the knowledge of God, as the waters cover the seas. (ISAIAH 11:9)

SOLOMON IBN GABIROL
SUBLIME POET

c. 1020–1057, SPAIN

He said: 'Everything requires a fence.'
He was asked, 'What kind of fence?'
He answered, 'Trust.'
'What is the fence of trust?' he was asked.
And he replied, 'Faith.'
To the further question, 'What is the fence of faith?'
he answered, 'To fear nothing.'

('The Choice of Pearls')

The Jewish presence in Moorish Andalusia (southern Spain) from the ninth to the twelfth centuries gave rise to a vibrant subculture exemplified by its Jewish literature and poetry. Solomon ibn Gabirol epitomized this Golden Age. Born in Malaga around 1020, by the age of sixteen he had earned himself a reputation as a fully fledged poet, famed for his attacks on injustice and the petty emptiness of daily life. His melancholy outlook, caused in good part by a lonely, parentless childhood and constant illness, drove Gabirol to his books and focused his attention on matters that he considered to be of true importance and worth. Just as the literary prophets of the Bible had influenced generations with their sublime language and poetry, so Gabirol used his poetic and philosophical writings to reprove his contemporaries and inspire them with his faith.

Gabirol spent most of his short life in Saragossa in northeast Spain, where he was educated in Arabic and Hebrew, and wrote hundreds of poems and philosophical works. His sophisticated religious language, heavily influenced by Arabic, celebrates the great mystery of God, reflecting Gabirol's belief that praise and worship are humanity's only appropriate response to God's greatness.

However, he also demanded redemption from God for his people. The fragile existence of the Jewish community in Muslim Spain was evidenced by the frequent murders of prominent Jews and the expulsion of anyone who was out of favour. When Gabirol's adored patron Yekutiel was executed in 1039, Gabirol's opponents forced him to leave Saragossa for fear of his literary outpourings of anger and condemnation. As a result he wrote *The Improvement of the Moral Qualities*, which includes discussions on pride, meekness, modesty and disrespect.

Gabirol's most famous philosophical work, *The Fountain of Life*, dares to consider the nature of humanity and its purpose. He contends that all existence is permeated with a yearning towards God, of which it is a part. Far from being insignificant grains of sand, human beings are therefore links in a great chain that leads ever upwards, striving to be nearer the Divine.

Gabirol died in Valencia at about the age of thirty-seven. He left a legacy of writings that give hope to all who read them and bring us closer to God. His religious poems, especially his penitential poems for Yom Kippur, can be found in Jewish prayer books even today.

NIGHT STORM

I am the man who has girded his loins
And will not pause till his oath is fulfilled
Whose divided heart wrestles with itself
Whose soul despises its fleshy home
Who chose, as a child, the path of wisdom
Even if Time's furnaces were to try him sevenfold
Uprooting what he plants, breaching his defence
Tearing down whatever he might build.
He will reach to the limits of wisdom and instruction
And probe what the mind's treasures hold

Despite the searing sorrows of misfortune
And the hurdles which Fate throws across his path.

('THE CHOICE OF PEARLS')

FAITH THROUGH LIFE

In the morning I look for you
My rock and my tower.
I lay my prayers before you
That day and night are in me.
Before your greatness I stand
And am unnerved
Because your eye will see
The thoughts that are in me.

What is it that the heart
Or the tongue can do
And what power is there
In the spirit that is in me?

But I know you are pleased
With the songs that
    men make
And so I shall praise you
While the divine soul is in me.

(PENITENTIAL PRAYER FOR YOM KIPPUR)

BACHYA IBN PAKUDA
SPIRITUAL GUIDE
ELEVENTH CENTURY, SPAIN

The aim and value of the duties of the heart
consist in their securing the equal co-operation
of body and soul in the service of God.
This harmony is called wholeheartedness.

(INTRODUCTION, 'DUTIES OF THE HEART')

Bachya ben Joseph ibn Pakuda is widely believed to have been one of the most popular Jewish authors of the Middle Ages. Surprisingly little is known about his life, but he was almost certainly a contemporary of Solomon ibn Gabirol and worked as a dayan (a judge of the rabbinical court) in Saragossa. It was in this culturally vibrant city, under Moorish rule, that he completed his influential work, *Duties of the Heart*, the first systematic presentation of Jewish ethics and spiritual growth.

As a dayan, Pakuda would have spent his days deliberating on the minutiae of Jewish ritual law, but outside this role (perhaps as an escape from it), he strove to refocus Judaism on the inner spiritual attitudes which he believed should determine religious life. Like so many prophets before him, his intention was to correct what he saw as an over-emphasis on ritual, a dependence which by Pakuda's time had developed into a pedantic and all-consuming absorption in Talmudic law and its interpretation. By reattaching value to the doer rather than to the deed alone, he sought to redress the balance and turn attention inwards, away from the external trappings of religious observance.

Pakuda's *Duties of the Heart*, written in Arabic around 1080, divides the obligations incumbent upon the religious person into 'Duties of the Limbs', those acts involving the body, and 'Duties of the Heart', those undertakings which involve a person's inner life, attitude or motivation. The Duties of the Limbs include various ritual and ethical observances commanded by the Torah, while the Duties of the Heart, divided into ten 'gates' or chapters, consist of beliefs and attitudes of spiritual trust, love and awe – those qualities that Pakuda believed determined the state of a person's soul and which he argued had been sorely neglected by other Jewish scholars.

In promoting a religion that transcends a mechanical fulfilment of the Commandments, Pakuda's chief concern was that Judaism should be a Torah of the heart. While medieval philosophers like Maimonides searched for proofs of God's existence, he offered people the means to grow through spiritual discipline and awareness. His *Duties of the Heart* became one of the Jewish world's best-loved ethical treatises, and has been translated into all the major languages of the Diaspora.

INWARD AND OUTWARD RELIGION

As the science of religion deals with two parts, external and inward religion, I studied the books of the ancient writers who flourished after the Talmud and who composed many works dealing with the Commandments, in the expectation of learning from them the science of inward religion. I found, however, that this department of knowledge, the science of the duties of the heart, had been entirely neglected. No work had been composed which set forth its principles and divisions systematically. I was so greatly surprised that I said to myself, 'possibly this class of duties is not positively enjoined by the Torah'. A careful examination, however, by the light of reason, scripture and tradition convinced me that they indeed form the foundation of all the Commandments, and that if there is any shortcoming in their observance, no external duties whatever can be properly fulfilled.

(INTRODUCTION, 'DUTIES OF THE HEART')

DISCERNING GOD'S WILL

A king wishing to test the intelligence of his servants distributed amongst them skeins of silk. The diligent and sensible one among them sorted the portion allocated to him again and again and divided it according to its quality into three parts – superfine, medium and inferior. With each of these he did the best that could be done with it and had the material made up by skilled workmen into gala dresses of different styles and colours which he wore in the Royal presence, selecting the garments suitable to the occasion and place. The fool among the king's servants made up of all the silk that which the wise servant had made out of the worst sort, sold it for whatever it would fetch and hastened to squander the proceeds in eating and drinking.

God too has given his servants the book of his true law in order to test them. The wise and sagacious man when he reads and clearly understands it will classify its contents under different heads. First he will endeavour to know the subtle spiritual themes which belong to the science of the inward life – the duties of the heart, the discipline of the soul – and will constrain himself continually to fulfil these duties. Then he will select the second part, namely the practical duties, which he will endeavour to perform each in its due time and place.

(INTRODUCTION, 'DUTIES OF THE HEART')

MOSES MAIMONIDES
MASTER TEACHER

1135–1204, EGYPT

There are those who set their thought to work to attain
perfection in the divine science, turn wholly towards
God and direct all acts of the intellect towards an
examination of God and God's beings. This is the
rank of the prophets.

('GUIDE OF THE PERPLEXED', III, 51)

No one since Moses has exercised as much influence and authority over Judaism as Rabbi Moses ben Maimon, known after the initial letters of his name as the RaMBaM. Maimonides was born in Cordova in 1135, but fled Spain with his family at the age of thirteen to escape Muslim persecution, eventually settling in Fostat near Cairo. He spent his early adult life immersed in Jewish learning and wrote his first major work, a commentary to the Mishnah – the code of Jewish law – in his twenties. Although financed during this time by his wealthy brother David, a dealer in precious stones, he was later forced to support himself when his brother drowned at sea. He chose to study medicine, eventually becoming personal physician to the Sultan's vizier. Still studying and writing in his spare time, he brought his enormous knowledge of Judaism to bear on the pressing issue of how to sustain the faith of the people, drawing on both the traditional sources and the disciplines of philosophy and science in his attempts. The lucidity and persuasiveness of his discourse and his penetrating way of dealing with legal argument gave him a unique ability to create coherence amongst the vast corpus of Jewish legal and ethical tenets, as demonstrated in his great code of Jewish law, the *Mishneh Torah*.

In his day, Maimonides was considered Judaism's foremost authority. He received letters from Jewish communities all over the world, seeking his opinions on belief, ritual and practice, and his messages of hope and wisdom offered in reply did much to sustain otherwise deprived and demoralized communities – just as Jeremiah's letters to the exiles in Babylon had done almost two thousand years before. But he was not without his critics, especially after his death. His use of Greek philosophy to shed light on Jewish teaching was frowned upon by some as heretical, and others considered his teachings dangerous because of the authority he assumed in codifying Jewish law. However, Maimonides' writings – especially his great philosophical treatise, the *Guide of the Perplexed* – remain an inspiration to Jews, Christians and Muslims who seek a religious faith based on reason. In this same vein of reason, Maimonides argued that prophecy is a natural state of being to which all can aspire. He maintained that when the human mind has sufficient intelligence and sensitivity along with courage and foresight, it can 'tune into' the divine insight that is prophecy. As such, Maimonides was a prophet and, indeed, considered himself to be so. He taught that prophecy is the summit of human achievement and the goal of all who hope for religious fulfilment.

PURPOSE OF THE LAW

The general object of the law is twofold: the well-being of the soul and the well-being of the body. The well-being of the soul is promoted by correct opinions communicated to the people according to their capacity. Some of these opinions are therefore imparted in a plain form, others allegorically because certain opinions are in their plain form too strong for the capacity of the common people. The well-being of the body is established by a proper management of the relations in which we live one to another. This we can attain in two ways: first by removing all violence from our midst, that is to say, that we do not do everyone as he pleases, desires and is able to do, but every one of us does that which contributes towards the common welfare. Secondly, by teaching every one of us such good morals as must produce a good social state. Of these two objects, the one of the well-being of the soul or the communication of correct opinions comes undoubtedly first in rank but the other, the well-being of the body, the Government of the State and the establishment of the best possible relations among men is anterior in nature and in time.

('GUIDE OF THE PERPLEXED', III, 27)

ON PROPHECY

Sometimes the truth flashes out to us so that we think that it is day and then matter and habit in their various forms conceal it so that we find ourselves again in an obscure night almost as we were at first. Among us there is one for whom the lightning flashes time and time again, so that he is always, as it were, in unceasing light. Thus night appears to him as day. That is the degree of the great one among the prophets, namely Moses, of whom it is written 'that the skin of his face sent forth beams' (Exodus 34:29). There are those to whom the lightning flashes only once in the whole of his life, that is the rank of those of whom it is said, 'They prophesised once but they did so no more' (Numbers 11:25). There are others between whose lightning flashes there are greater or shorter intervals.

('GUIDE OF THE PERPLEXED',

INTRODUCTION TO PART I)

ISAAC ABRAVANEL
COURAGEOUS DEFENDER OF THE FAITH
1437–1508, SPAIN

The revelation which comes to the prophet and which is received by his intellect is not produced by him, but is in accord with that which has been taught to him by heaven.

(COMMENTARY ON MAIMONIDES' 'GUIDE OF THE PERPLEXED' II:36)

In the spring of 1492, the Catholic King Ferdinand and Queen Isabella of Spain ordered the expulsion of all Jewish people from their lands – effectively bringing to an end with a single edict the cultural achievements of Spanish Jewry that had enriched European civilization for over five hundred years.

Financier and Jewish philosopher Don Isaac Abravanel was in no way shielded from the growing anti-Jewish sentiment in the kingdom, despite his esteemed position as state treasurer. He offered huge sums for the edict of expulsion to be revoked, but was ultimately rejected by the authorities he had served so well. Faced with exile, he steadfastly refused to convert to Christianity and chose instead, as Leo Baeck would in his time, to offer comfort and hope to the people in their final days of suffering. His loyalty to Judaism and God served as a courageous example to his co-religionists, encouraging them to stand firm in their own faith and refuse the conversion to Christianity forced upon them through the Inquisition.

Having repudiated its government, Abravanel left Spain with the responsibility of finding homes for more than a hundred and fifty thousand stateless and impoverished Jews. He himself eventually found sanctuary in Naples, where he settled into a life of study and a new position as financial adviser to the king. It was here that he wrote his works on political philosophy and his biblical commentary. Drawing on the works of both Jewish and Christian thinkers and absorbing the ideas of the Renaissance, he introduced humanism into Jewish thought. In spite of his experience of bigotry and persecution, he held to a prophetic vision of a just and religiously tolerant society, headed by a regularly elected government, accountable to all. In this rationalistic spirit, he saw the biblical prophets not so much as seers but as great figures of universal humanism – visionary leaders who had laid down the building blocks of a moral society by taking God's message to their own people in their own time.

Don Isaac Abravanel shouldered great public responsibility, but he also endured the personal humiliations of the Jewish people living in medieval times. He became a symbol of the people as he was alternately honoured, rejected and exiled. He also exemplified the Jewish people's spiritual resistance with his unfailing love of knowledge and truth and his pursuit of justice. His hopes for a fairer world have, to some extent, come to pass in the modern age, but he was not to see these visions in his lifetime. He died in Venice in 1508, mourned by the leaders of the republic and the entire Jewish community.

DEMOCRATIC LEADERSHIP

We are required to know whether a monarch is a necessity, inherently needed for the people, or whether it is possible to exist without one. If people think that government must be based on three things –

unity, continuity and power – then the necessity of a monarch is fallacious. For it is not impracticable that a people should have many leaders, united, agreeing and concurring in one counsel who can decide administrative and judicial matters. Then why should not their administration be for one or three years or less than that!

It is more likely that one man should trespass, through his folly or strong temptations or anger, than that many

*men taking counsel should trespass. For if one of them turns aside
from the right path, the others will protest against him. Moreover
since their administration is temporary and they must render
account after a short while, the fear of men will be upon them.*

(COMMENTARY ON DEUTERONOMY 17:14)

SOURCE OF TRUE WISDOM

*All these commentaries and works I wrote after I had left my country.
Before that, all the time that I had was in the courts and palaces of the
kings, engaged in their service. I had no leisure for study and looked
at no book, but spent my days in vanity and my years in trouble in
getting riches and honour; and now those very riches have perished by
evil adventure and the glory is departed from Israel. It was only after
I had become a fugitive and a wanderer on the earth, from one
kingdom to another, and without money, that I sought out the book of
God. . . . I have limited myself in my old age to the contemplation
of* The Guide of the Perplexed *[of Maimonides] and to the exposition of
the Bible. These are the sources of all knowledge and in their wisdom
all doubts and perplexities are dissolved.*

(LETTER TO SAUL HACOHEN ASHKENAI, VENICE, 1507)

DONA GRACIA MENDES
VALIANT ACTIVIST

1510–1569, PORTUGAL

The intrinsic piety of Miriam offering her life to save her brethren, the great prudence of Deborah in governing her people, the infinite virtue and great sanctity of Esther in helping those who are persecuted and the much praised strength of the most chaste and magnanimous Judith.

(SAMUEL USQUE, DEDICATORY ADDRESS TO DONA GRACIA IN

'CONSOLATION FOR THE TRIBULATIONS OF ISRAEL')

Dona Gracia Mendes was born in Portugal with the Christian name of Beatrice de Luna. As a Marrano, she was brought up in an ostensibly Catholic family, which secretly abided by the Jewish beliefs of its ancestors: members of the household therefore attended mass regularly but rested behind closed doors on the Sabbath, abstained from foods forbidden by Jewish law and fasted covertly on Yom Kippur.

Sixteenth-century Catholic society was becoming increasingly hostile towards its Marrano population, however, and the Mendes lived in constant fear of being exposed as secret Jews. By 1536, the Inquisition was officially established in Portugal, with the terrifying result that many Marranos were burned at the stake for heresy. When Gracia was widowed at the age of twenty-six, she decided to escape from Portugal and travelled with her baby daughter to her brother-in-law's house in Antwerp. There, she helped set up an 'underground network' of agents in England, Flanders, France and Germany to help other Marranos to escape. The city of Antwerp was within the control of the Inquisition, but Gracia acted fearlessly in overseeing the passage of hundreds of persecuted souls to safety.

Gracia moved cities again in 1544 – this time to avoid her daughter's engagement to a local Catholic nobleman. In Ferrara in northern Italy, finally safe from the Inquisition, she was able to openly admit her Judaism for the first time in her life. No less committed to the plight of her co-religionists, she took the new name of Gracia Mendes of the House of Nasi (her Jewish familial name) and continued to help the Marranos. But like Jeremiah before her, Gracia's uncompromising stance was considered to be a direct threat to the stability of nations, and she was arrested during a visit to Venice for 'Judaising activities'. On her release, she settled in Turkey, where she commissioned the first translation of the Bible into Spanish ('The Ferrara Bible'), intended for Marranos who were unable to read Hebrew.

In 1556, twenty-five Marranos were arrested in Ancona, Italy, and burned at the stake. Ever swift to take action, Mendes organized a boycott of Ancona's port by Jewish merchants all over the world. Unfortunately, the protest failed as some rabbinic authorities were afraid to give religious approval for such direct action. Dona Gracia was bitterly disappointed at her people's failure to take action against injustice. All her life she demonstrated that political and economic protest could be at least as, or more effective than, the traditional paths of prayer and petitions. Her many achievements show that it is not always necessary for Jews to suffer injury passively.

REDEMPTION OF CAPTIVES

In such wise with her golden arm and heavenly grasp, she raised most of this people from the depths of this and other infinite travails in which they were kept enthralled in Europe by poverty and sin; she brings them to safe lands and does not cease to guide them and gather them to the obedience and precepts of their God of old. Thus she has been your tried strength in your weakness, a bank where the weary rest; a fountain of clear water where the parched drink; a fruit-laden shady tree where the hungry eat and the desolate find respite, more particularly, she was spared of that great succour, and remains at all times a tried relief in all the miseries of the Portuguese people – a strong column to support many who were once prisoner and to help them with their own fortune.

(SAMUEL USQUE, 'CONSOLATION FOR THE TRIBULATIONS OF ISRAEL')

SAVING THE PEOPLE

The Jewish people would have been entirely lost had not God raised up for them a remnant of the house of Nasi who made smooth the path of fugitives who wished to return to their God. She stood at the roadside in the tent of Abraham to receive their groaning wayfarers who return to the service of their creator so tired and weary that every knee would have faltered but for this great house, which was appointed from heaven to have mercy upon them. Every soul of the house of Jacob that comes to take refuge under the pinions of her divine presence, she was their mother and suckled them from her comforting breast.

(SAADIAH LUNGO OF SALONCIA, ELEGY TO DONA GRACIA, 1569)

MANASSEH BEN ISRAEL
HOPE OF ISRAEL

1604–1657, HOLLAND

*Truly we men do draw so much the nearer to Divine
nature, when by so much we cherish and defend the
small and weak ones. And with how much diligence
do we perform this?*

('THE HOPE OF ISRAEL', 1650)

The Jewish world in the seventeenth century was marked by the continued outpouring of Marranos from Spain and Portugal following the Catholic edict of expulsion and the persecution of the Inquisition. These Marranos (forced converts to Catholicism), who miraculously had maintained a secret adherence to Judaism over two generations, were now beginning to emerge as Jews. Like Jewish people all over Europe, they yearned to settle in new lands free from religious persecution.

Manasseh ben Israel, himself a former Marrano, was determined to find a way to secure the liberty of the Jewish people and ensure the future of Judaism. As a communal rabbi in Amsterdam and a leading Hebrew scholar, he corresponded with Jews and non-Jews all over the world in an effort to find a solution to the desperate plight of the Jewish refugees. Although ridiculed, and eventually disowned by his Amsterdam community for his stubborn single-mindedness, he made this his life's work and did much to lessen the suffering of the Jewish people.

Manasseh believed that by leading the efforts to help the refugees he was answering God's call. He was a pragmatist and political strategist when dealing with governments and statesmen, but he nonetheless kept before him a prophetic vision of the justice of his cause and the plight of the disenfranchised and stateless. He also believed that his work had messianic implications – for only if the Jews were dispersed throughout the countries of the world, and to England in

particular, as the 'angle terre' (the 'end of the earth', according to Manasseh's translation), would the Messiah return to lead them back to the Holy Land as prophesied by Daniel in the Bible (Daniel 12:7). His tireless entreaties, made on behalf of the entire Jewish nation, established ideas of religious freedom and tolerance for minorities and refugees, and set in motion the practice of Jewish national diplomacy to be emulated two centuries later by the Zionist leader Theodor Herzl.

To support the settlement of Jews in England, from where they had been officially banned since 1290, Manasseh dedicated the Latin edition of his work, *The Hope of Israel*, to the English Parliament in 1650. He continued to campaign for the formal acceptance of Jewish settlement in England until his death, famously appearing before Oliver Cromwell in 1655 to argue his case. His endeavours, as well as giving hope to Jews everywhere, initiated an unofficial acceptance of his petition, which eventually led to the granting of an official charter of protection to the Jews of England in 1664, seven years after his death.

THE WORTH OF JEWISH IMMIGRANTS

Three things, if it please your highness, there are that make a strange nation well-beloved amongst the natives of a land where they dwell (as the defect of these three things make them hateful): profit they may receive from them, fidelity they hold towards their princes and the nobleness and purity of their blood. Now when I shall have made good, that all these three things are found in the Jewish nation, I shall certainly persuade your Highness, that with a favourable eye you shall be pleased to receive again the nation of the Jews, who in time past lived in that Island but I know not by what false informations, were cruelly handled and banished. . . . From hence it results that the Jewish nation, though scattered throughout the whole world, are not therefore a despisable people, but as a plant worthy to be

planted in the whole world, and received into populous cities; who ought to plant them in those places which are most secure from danger, being trees of most savoury fruit.

('The Humble Address of Manasseh ben Israel to Oliver Cromwell')

MESSIANIC REDEMPTION

For I have conceived that our universal dispersion was a necessary circumstance, to be fulfilled, before all that shall be accomplished which God has promised to the people of the Jews concerning their restoration and their returning again into their own land, according to the words of the prophet Daniel 12:7, 'When the scattering of the power of the holy people comes to an end, all these things shall be fulfilled.' As also, that this, our scattering, little by little should be from the one end of the earth even to the other, as it is written in Deuteronomy 28:64. I conceived by the end of the earth might be understood this island. And I knew not, but God, who often works by natural means might have designed and made choice of me for the bringing about this work.

('Defense of Judaism', Seventh Section, 1656)

BARUKH SPINOZA
DEFENDER OF TRUTH
1632–1677, HOLLAND

By the help of God, I mean the fixed and unchangeable order of Nature or the chain of natural events which always involve eternal truth and necessity.

('THEOLOGICAL-POLITICAL TRACTATE', CHAPTER 3)

Like his ancient prophetic forebears, the medieval philosopher Barukh Spinoza was a passionate critic of religious rituals which, he argued, were practised not for the service of God but only for the satisfaction of the people. His controversial opinions were met with considerable alarm by his Amsterdam community, who understood them to be a direct attack on the traditions and essence of the Judaism of his day. To silence Spinoza – and no doubt also fearful of the effect such 'heresy' would have on their Christian hosts – the rabbis served the 23-year-old with a *cherem* (a ban of excommunication) in 1656, forcing him to spend the rest of his days seeking God's truth outside any religious tradition.

Although an outcast, Spinoza continued to adhere to Jewish ideas, drawing especially on the teachings of Maimonides, such as his refusal to define God in any particularistic way and his belief in God's presence in all creation. Spinoza argued that God is the only substance in the world and that everything else is merely a constituent part. According to this philosophy, all things created have an order and meaning, but God cannot be viewed as a supernatural moral authority. Human beings are not captives of external forces – rather, as we reach rational understanding, our ideas become part of the infinite idea of God. A good society, in Spinoza's view, is therefore one that allows rational beings to think freely and, for this society to flourish, there must be civil order and peace in a state of religious freedom and democracy. In this way, Spinoza outlined his vision of

a free and tolerant society, which has since become the model of the modern nation state.

Spinoza remained independent in his thinking and writings, and lived out his exiled days in the Hague, earning a meagre living grinding and polishing optical lenses. His understanding of truth was dependent on the individual rather than the community, but he must have cut a lonely prophetic figure as he sought and defended a new understanding of God's world. Despite his alienation from the Jewish community, and the ambiguity with which the Jewish community has regarded him ever since, he continued to develop the biblical notion of humanity's ability to reflect God's image and fulfil God's will. As God has endowed us with a conscience and ability to reason, so Spinoza believed we have the power to create a universal ethic and a moral society.

ON GOD IN NATURE

To say that everything happens according to natural laws and to say that everything is ordained by the decree and ordinance of God, is the same thing. Now since the power in Nature is identical with the power of God, by which alone all things happen and are determined, it follows that whatsoever man, as a part of nature, provides himself with to aid and preserve his existence, or whatsoever Nature affords him, without his help, is given solely by the Divine power.

('THEOLOGICAL-POLITICAL TRACTATE', CHAPTER 3)

ON RELIGION

Ambition and unscrupulousness have waxed so powerful that religion is thought to consist not so much in respecting the Holy writings as in defending human commentaries, so that religion is no longer identified with charity, but with spreading discord and propagating intense hatred disguised under the name of zeal for God and eager ardour. To these evils we must add superstition, which teaches men to despise reason and Nature. If we would separate ourselves from the crowd, we must consider the true method of interpreting scripture, which should not differ widely from the method of interpreting nature.

('THEOLOGICAL-POLITICAL TRACTATE', CHAPTER 7)

DEMOCRACY

The basis and aim of a democracy is to bring men as far as possible under the control of reason, so that they may live in peace and harmony. If this basis be removed, the whole fabric falls to ruin. It will perhaps be thought that we are turning citizens into slaves, for slaves obey commands and free men live as they like; but this idea is based in a misconception, for the true slave is he who is led away by his pleasures and can neither see what is good for him, nor act accordingly; he alone is free who lives with free consent under the entire guidance of reason. . . . I think I have now shown sufficiently clearly the basis of a democracy. I have especially desired to do so, for I believe it to be of all forms of government, the most natural and the most consonant with individual liberty. In it no one transfers his natural right so absolutely that he has no further voice in affairs; he only hands it over to the majority of a society, whereof he is a unit. Thus all men remain, as they were in the state of Nature, equals.

('THEOLOGICAL-POLITICAL TRACTATE', CHAPTER 16)

BAAL SHEM TOV
CHARISMATIC MYSTIC

1698–1760, POLAND

A father complained to the Besht [Baal Shem Tov]
that his son had forsaken God. 'What, Rabbi, shall I do?'
'Love him more than ever,' was the Besht's reply.

(RABBI DOV BAER, 'IN PRAISE OF THE BAAL SHEM TOV')

Born Israel ben Eliezer in 1698, the charismatic spiritual leader Baal Shem Tov studied the ideas of Kabbalah (Jewish mysticism) as a young teacher in Poland. In marked contrast to the rabbis and scholars of the period, who preferred to wrangle over the minutiae of Jewish law, Israel understood and sympathized with the problems faced by the common people. Following the ancient prophets' abhorrence of empty ritual, he advocated simplicity in learning and in piety, believing that excessive attention to legal argument was a barrier to *Kavvanah* (concentration of the mind). He once said of a scholar, 'I envy him his scholarship but what am I to do? I have no time to study because I am under compulsion to serve my Maker.' As Judaism became steadily more unresponsive to human needs, his influence grew: by about 1735, he was established as a charismatic faith healer who could perform miracle cures and foretell the future. He acquired the Kabbalistic title 'Baal Shem Tov' ('Master of the Good Name'), often abbreviated to the Besht, in acknowledgement of the belief that he had unlocked the secret of God's hidden name and its attendant supernatural powers.

The resulting Hasidic movement (from the Hebrew *hasidut*, meaning piety) soon spread throughout Eastern Europe. As its prototype *zaddik* (spiritual leader), the Besht attained a holy status in the eyes of his followers, and stories of his teaching and methods were widespread. The Besht believed it was his divine mission to bring happiness and meaning to the lives of the people, advising, 'You are righteous when you feel more joy in cleaving to God than any material pleasure.' Hasidism emphasized ecstasy and enthusiasm as a means of showing devotion. Contemplating the omnipresence of the Divine, the *hasid* (Hasidic follower) seeks to attain unity with God through intense concentration and the abandonment of self. Each hasid has a spiritual guide (a *rebbe* or *zaddik*) who leads them on their journey of faith, and who is said to have the power to intervene in divine affairs on behalf of his followers.

Despite concerted rabbinic attempts to stem its popularity, Hasidism became an established way of life in Eastern Europe and developed into the influential Jewish movement it is today. Its many eighteenth-century opponents feared that it would lead to the creation of false prophets and undermine the traditional Jewish way of life. In fact, the movement is credited with injecting much-needed vitality into a faith that had become rigid and static. As its founder, the Besht brought great comfort to the poor and oppressed he cared about so passionately, and enlivened Judaism with renewed devotion and enthusiasm for God's work on earth.

TRUE FAITH

The Besht commented on the phrase in the prayer book: 'Our God and the God of our ancestors.' He said, 'Some people have faith because their ancestors taught them to believe. In one sense this is satisfactory, no philosophical arguments will break their belief; in another sense, it is unsatisfactory, since their belief does not come from personal knowledge. Others come to belief through conviction after research. This is satisfactory in one sense, they know God from inner conviction; in another sense, it is unsatisfactory: if others demonstrate to them the fallacy of their reasoning, they may become unbelievers. The best believers are those whose beliefs are satisfactory in every way; they believe because of tradition and also through their own reasoning. This is what we mean when we say:

"Our God and God of our ancestors." God is our master both because we know it and because our ancestors taught us.'

('IN PRAISE OF THE BAAL SHEM TOV')

TRUE DEVOTION

The Besht was about to enter a synagogue but he halted at the door and exclaimed: 'This place is overfilled with prayers and learning.' 'Why then do you hesitate to enter such a holy place?' inquired his disciples. 'Were this a truly holy place,' replied the Besht, 'the prayer and learning would have ascended upwards to heaven and the synagogue would be empty of them. Only the prayer and learning which does not come from the heart can fill an earthly abode.'

('IN PRAISE OF THE BAAL SHEM TOV')

THE SPIRITUAL SEARCH

A farmer held up an egg in his hand and mused, 'I shall place this egg under a hen, I shall raise up the chick and it shall hatch other chicks. I will sell them and purchase a cow and . . .' While planning thus, he squeezed the egg and it broke in his fingers. In the same fashion some people are satisfied in the sum of their holiness and knowledge they have attained and think constantly that they are superior to others. But they do not perceive that by doing this they lose even the little they have attained.

('IN PRAISE OF THE BAAL SHEM TOV')

HANNAH WERBERMACHER
SPIRITUAL HEALER

1815–1892, UKRAINE

*I have just returned from the heavenly court
where I received a new and sublime soul.*

('HANNAH WERBERMACHER' IN S. A. HORODEZKY, 'LEADERS OF HASIDISM')

Hannah Werbermacher is described in accounts of the time as *isha kesherah* (a pious woman), with an ability to foretell the future. The only child of a well-to-do and educated businessman, she was born in 1815 in the Ukrainian town of Ludomir. She took to reading the Bible at any early age and soon learned to write Hebrew, progressing from this to study the Talmudic literature and Halachah (Jewish law). As a girl, her intense dedication to study raised some concern in the community, and she distinguished herself still further by her piety, performing ecstatic acts of prayer three times a day.

When Hannah came of age, she was betrothed to a young man with whom she had grown up – and whom, according to Jewish custom, she was not allowed to see until the wedding. It was also around this time that her mother died. Troubled and alone, she chose to cut herself off completely, leaving the house only to visit her mother's grave. During one such outing, she fell into a deep unconsciousness and, on recovery, announced herself endowed with a new and elevated soul. Henceforth, she gave herself utterly to religious life, breaking off her engagement and adopting the complete Jewish observance normally reserved for men.

Werbermacher built a synagogue next to her house and soon acquired a reputation for saintliness and miracle working. Men and women from the neighbouring areas, among them scholars and rabbis, flocked to receive healing from the 'holy maid of Ludomir'. As Jewish law demands of women, she would not allow anyone to see her, but addressed each visitor with blessings and dispensed curative herbs to the sick from behind a partially opened door. As her popularity as a *zaddik* (Hasidic leader) and spiritual healer grew, however, other Hasidic leaders in the region became wary of her influence and persuaded her to marry. She was divorced shortly afterwards, but this interruption to her life of seclusion appears to have dissipated her powers of healing and teaching. She spent her last years in the Holy Land, attempting through Kabbalah (Jewish mysticism) to bring about the coming of the Messiah.

As a woman prophet, Hannah Werbermacher was a revolutionary, challenging the male establishment and the exclusive claim of men to act as spiritual leaders in Hasidism – she is still the only woman known to have received the title of *zaddik*. Taking God's message to the people, she pioneered a new understanding of both spiritual and physical healing through Jewish teaching and blessing.

THE SPIRIT GROWS

Chana Rochel [Hannah Werbermacher] realized that she tapped the wellspring of her identity and powers not from what she wasn't, not by contrasting, but simply by being who she was, a creation of the Will of God. A manifestation of the Divine Intelligence. 'I am grateful that God created me as I am.' What a revelation. What simplicity of absolute faith and being.

As the years wore on, Chana Rochel grew stronger and more confident of herself and her role as rebbe. She was indeed possessed by a soul, her own soul. Let the world think what it might; she would continue to do just as she had been doing. Time had enabled Chana Rochel to respect herself as an individual blessed with the

*skill and insight to help others on their spiritual journeys. She
taught them how to overcome the various obstacles in their paths.
She taught herself, meanwhile, that there was no need to answer
those who would judge her, and now, rather than living defensively,
she began to direct her life with fortitude and deep personal faith.*

('The Maiden of Ludomir', from Gershon Winkler, 'They Called Her Rebbe')

EVEN IN OUR OWN TIME

Prophetic voices continue to be heard, crying out against injustice and urging us to uphold the moral law, and to recognize the sacred nature of our lives. Activists such as Henrietta Szold, Lily Montagu, Stephen S. Wise and David Ben-Gurion dedicated themselves wholeheartedly to social and ethical improvement. Each brought a religious, spiritual zeal to their vocation, but from outside established religious communal life or its practices. Their spirituality only knew of holiness in people and principles. They were attacked for their absolute dedication to their beliefs, but their legacy of noble work lives on.

By contrast, idealist prophets such as Theodor Herzl, Rav Kook, Martin Buber and Abraham Joshua Heschel drew on their ancient heritage and the ethical quality of religious life, and inspired and taught through their thinking and literary works. However, like their ancient forebears, these prophets took action too, often with a courage that did not come naturally to them.

Many prophetic heroes of our time were prepared to sacrifice their lives for the message that they practised and preached. They exemplify the noblest quality of humanity. At the world's darkest hour, Janusz Korczak and Leo Baeck offered hope and demonstrated that goodness can flourish. We reap the fruits of the work of these activists, idealists and heroes as we live out the prophetic tradition.

And God said to me, Go, prophesy to My people Israel. And so hear the word of God. (AMOS 7:15–16)

THEODOR HERZL
FATHER OF THE JEWISH STATE
1860–1904, AUSTRIA

If you will it, it is no dream.

(Author's Epigraph, 'Altneuland')

Herzl was working as a journalist for the Viennese newspaper *Neue Frie Presse* when, in 1891, he was sent to Paris to cover the notorious Dreyfus Affair. The case against the French army captain Dreyfus, though false, had provoked a storm of virulent anti-Semitism throughout France. Herzl was shocked into the realization that the 'Emancipation of the Jews' earlier in the nineteenth century had simply created a new tension, meaning that European Jews were again considered the outsiders they had been in medieval times. Herzl concluded that his people's only hope was to re-establish their homeland in Palestine – then under Turkish rule – and, through this, control of their own destiny. He published his views in *Der Judenstaat* ('The Jewish State') in 1896, noting in his diaries of the time, 'I do not remember ever having written anything in such an exalted state of mind as this book. . . . I heard the pinions of an eagle fluttering over my head as I wrote it.'

Despite considerable opposition, Herzl worked passionately for the establishment of a Jewish state from that moment on. Both Orthodox and Reform wings of the religious establishment were against political Zionism, the Reform arguing that the Jewish people were long settled in the lands of the Diaspora. Added

to his critics were those Jews who had so recently won emancipation in Western Europe, now fearful that Herzl's Zionist ideals would stir up a backlash and force them back into the ghettos. In those countries, primarily in Eastern Europe, where Jews continued to be openly discriminated against, however, Herzl became a revered symbol of freedom. His was a utopian vision and he pursued it relentlessly, meeting with leaders of many nations, and he was eventually recognized as a representative of Jewish people worldwide.

Herzl was elected president of the World Zionist Organization in Basle in 1897, and published *Alteneuland*, his dream of a Jewish state in an 'old new land', not long afterwards. It was with prophetic accuracy that he commented in his diaries, 'At Basle, I founded the Jewish state. If I were to say this today, I would be met with universal laughter. In five years and certainly in fifty, everyone will see it.' Herzl persuaded many with his fervour – although his vision was to prove problematic in its failure to address the question of Palestine's Arab communities. Unable ultimately to reach agreement with the Sultan of Turkey regarding Jewish settlement, he proposed the idea of a Jewish colony in East Africa as a sanctuary for the victims of the pogroms in Russia. The suggestion met with violent opposition within the Zionist movement, and Herzl died a disappointed man at an early age. He was buried in Vienna in 1904, but his remains were transported in 1949 – as requested in his will – to the newly established Jewish homeland that had been his dream and ambition. Revered by all, he was interred on what is now called Mount Herzl, the resting place of the founders of the Jewish state.

RESTORATION OF A JEWISH STATE

I am introducing no new idea; on the contrary, it is a very old one. It is a universal idea – and therein lies its power – as old as the people, which never, even in the time of bitterest calamity, ceased to cherish it. This is the restoration of the Jewish State. It is remarkable that the Jews should have dreamt this kingly dream all through the long night of our history. Now day is dawning. We need only rub the sleep out of our eyes, stretch our limbs and convert the dream into a reality. Though neither prophet nor visionary, I confess I cherish the

*hope and belief that the Jewish people will one day be fired by a
splendid enthusiasm. I shall take my part in it, in the ranks of those
friends and fellow workers whom I am endeavouring to arouse and
unite for a common cause.*

('THE JEWISH STATE: A SOLUTION TO THE JEWISH QUESTION', JEWISH CHRONICLE, 1896)

ONE PEOPLE

*We are one people – our enemies have made us one whether we will
it or not, as has repeatedly happened in history. Affliction binds us
together and thus united, we suddenly discover our strength. Yes, we
are strong enough to form a State and a model state. Every man may
test its truth for himself, for every man will carry with him a portion
of the Promised Land – one in his head, another in his arms, another
in his acquired possessions. We shall live at last, as free men, on our
own soil and die peacefully in our own homes.*

('THE JEWISH STATE: A SOLUTION TO THE JEWISH QUESTION', JEWISH CHRONICLE, 1896)

JEWISH DESTINY

*There is no more splendid work to be done in the preparation of the
Jewish people for its coming destiny. The students of today are to
become journeymen and master craftsmen and are to relieve us who
are actively at work today, in the work of Zionism. One time I called
Zionism an ideal that had no end. And I truly believe that Zionism
will not stop being an ideal even after the attainment of our land in
Palestine. For in Zionism, as I understand it, there is
contained not only the striving for a legally assured
homeland for our poor people but also the striving for
moral and spiritual perfection.*

('OUR HOPE' MAGAZINE, VIENNA, 1904)

HENRIETTA SZOLD
DEDICATED MOTHER OF ISRAEL

1860–1945, PALESTINE

If you wish to know what is meant by the ethics of
Judaism, search within the conscience of Henrietta Szold.
If you wish to gain an insight into the Jewish conscience,
listen to her voice, a voice inspired by the lightnings
of Sinai and the prophets of Israel.

(JUDAH MAGNES, PRESIDENT OF THE HEBREW UNIVERSITY, MEMORIAL TO HENRIETTA SZOLD,
20 FEBRUARY, 1945)

Henrietta Szold realized her capacity for selfless devotion at the age of twenty-one, when the first waves of poor and ignorant Jewish immigrants fleeing from the Russian pogroms found their way to her native Baltimore in the 1880s. The desperate plight of her Russian brethren triggered an outpouring of service and a call to duty in Szold that was to remain with her for the rest of her life. Well educated and privileged herself, she organized night classes for the immigrants and did all she could to assist their absorption into American life, thereby establishing a model for all future immigrant assimilation into the United States. Her knowledge of Jewish persecution led Szold to the conclusion that Zionism – the establishment of a Jewish homeland in Palestine – could be the only balm capable of healing the wounds that history had inflicted on the Jewish people.

In pursuit of this Zionist ideal, Szold visited Palestine in 1909, and was immediately captivated by the country's beauty and historical resonance. But she was also alarmed by the appalling standards of sanitation and medical care she encountered. Szold returned to the United States determined to found Hadassah, the women's organization that quickly developed into the largest Zionist body in

the world. One of Hadassah's first undertakings was to build the renowned Hadassah hospital in Jerusalem.

Although she preceded the Jewish feminist movement, Szold's pioneering achievements in public life have served as an inspiration to Jewish women everywhere. As early as 1916 she took the radical stance of insisting that she recite the Kaddish (mourner's prayer), traditionally recited by male children, for her mother. Her letter to Haym Peretz explaining this decision is treasured as an eloquent and moving appeal for equal rights. After emigrating to Palestine in 1920, she became a member of the Yishuv (the Jewish community's governing council) and was the first woman to be elected on to the Jewish Agency executive. In her later years, she organized Youth Aliyah, an ambitious movement that saved more than 30,000 children from certain murder by the Nazis, and settled them in kibbutzim and children's villages in Palestine.

Szold was a woman of great organizational ability and she used this skill in the service of Jewish children and the creation of a new society in an 'old-new land'. She did not live to see the formation of the state of Israel, but she made a unique contribution to its establishment, its hope for peace through the creation of a moral society, and its commitment to the health and social welfare of all its citizens.

WOMEN'S RIGHTS TO TRADITION

It is impossible for me to find words in which to tell you how deeply I was touched by your offer to act as 'Kaddish' for my dear mother. You will wonder then that I cannot accept your offer. The Kaddish means to me that the survivor publicly and markedly manifests his wish and intention to assume the relationship to the Jewish community, which his parent had, and that so the chain of tradition remains unbroken from generation to generation, each adding its own link. You can do that for the generations of your family, I must do that for the generations of my family. I believe that the elimination of women from such duties was never intended by our laws and custom – women were freed from positive duties when they could not perform them, but not when they could. It was never intended, that if they could perform them, their performance of them should not be considered as valuable and valid as when one of the male sex performed them. And of the Kaddish I feel sure this is particularly true.

(LETTER TO HAYM PERETZ, NEW YORK, 16 SEPTEMBER, 1916)

A HOLY LAND, A HOLY PEOPLE

As one carrying responsibility for more than 7,300 boys and girls, I venture to address myself herewith to the leaders of the Jewish community in Palestine. Intolerance bids fair to prevail. Men who express views at variance with those of a presumed majority are exposed to bodily harm. Political scores are settled with bombs. Licence is tending to replace law among the people of the law. Liberty of conscience and freedom of speech threaten to slip away from our guardianship. Our hallowed ethical standards are in danger of declining. These are evil things of which our camp must be cleansed. The young warrior builders fulfilling our behest to fight against totalitarianism and the mothers of our future; hosts of peace, freedom and justice demand of us to be mindful of the teaching of our people's history. The Jew and his cause have persisted through the ages not by might of the fist, nor by the power of brute force, but by the spirit of divine law and love.

(ADDRESS TO THE YISHUV, JERUSALEM, 1942)

RAV KOOK
SPIRITUAL LEADER
1865–1935, PALESTINE

The truly righteous complain not of wickedness
but multiply justice; complain not of a denial of faith,
but multiply faith; complain not of ignorance
but multiply wisdom.

('ARPELE TOHAR')

Rav Avraham Kook was born in Latvia and studied at the famous Yeshiva (Jewish Academy) of Volozhyn. As a committed religious Zionist, he felt a deep mystical connection to the land of Israel, and moved there in 1904 to become Chief Rabbi of Jaffa. In 1919 he was appointed Ashkenazi Chief Rabbi of Jerusalem and in 1921, became the first Chief Rabbi of Palestine. Kook believed that he was gifted with a holy spirit and, like the ancient prophets before him, saw himself as a channel by which the light of God could reach out to the world. His intense desire to kindle the sparks of faith in all motivated him to work with the secular Zionist groups, engaged in building new national institutions, as well as with the religious communities in Palestine, which were deeply opposed to the establishment of a secular nation state in the Holy Land. Impressing all parties with his openness and tolerance, he became widely respected for his learning and faith, even by those who decried any religion.

Kook's influence on the structure of the Jewish state, the first since Yohanan ben Zakkai's time, is still felt today. In negotiation with David Ben-Gurion, the first Israeli Prime Minister, he worked to achieve a balance between the religious and the secular in the state's governance, adhering to traditional Jewish law wherever this was possible. When issues arose where the traditional interpretation of the law seemed to pose undue hardship, Kook reinterpreted the law for the sake of equity, especially with regard to the ancient laws concerning use of the land. He was criticized by some for this flexibility but his reputation as a scholar of the highest repute, driven by the best interests of all concerned, ensured that he continued to act as spiritual leader of his people.

As a scholar Kook wrote about the bewilderment of humanity in the modern world and its need for guidance. Like the medieval thinker Bachya ibn Pakuda, he believed that Judaism had concentrated for too long on the study of texts and the Commandments, at the expense of a more mystical, inner appreciation of the divine. His independent spirit brought him many adversaries, and he placed himself at the centre of controversy by insisting that Jewish law had a part to play in the creation of a modern nation state. At the same time, he effectively transcended political nationalism with his obvious piety and his efforts to elevate the modern Jewish state to 'a kingdom of priests and a holy nation' (Exodus 19:6).

SERVING GOD AND PEOPLE

Your honour is fortunate that he is privileged to be free of the burden of public service and he can withdraw and pursue the truth in its full perfection. But I am deprived being burdened all day with the responsibilities of serving those people of God. My only delight is that I remind myself that my feet are stationed on the holy soil, on the land God has called his portion and his inheritance and characterized with various expressions of endearment. If someone gave me all the land in the world, it would not compare with one moment of breathing the holy air of Eretz Israel (Land of Israel). I trust in Him to help me for the honour of his name, that no stumbling results from my work and that I never pronounce anything against His will.

(LETTER TO RABBI JOSEPH DAVID, 'IGGEROT HA RE'AYAH', VOL. I, LETTER 602, 1962–5)

THE HOLY NATION IN ITS LAND

The sounds of song, the majesty of the holy tongue, the beauty of our precious land, which was chosen by God, the ecstasy of heroism and holiness will return to the mountains of Zion. With the cleansing potency of the original soul of our people, with hidden divine influences and with the light of mercy will they come and cleanse all the outer garments in which the soul and spirit of the nation robed itself. 'And you will dwell in the land I gave to your ancestors and you will be my people and I will be your God' (Ezekiel 36:28).

('The Soul of Nationhood and Its Body')

STRENGTHENING THE PEOPLE

The natural fear of sin in the general area of morals is the healthiest expression of human nature. It is the singular characteristic of the nature of the Jew in reacting to every form of wrongdoing that violates the Torah and the commandments, the heritage of the community of Jacob. This disposition will not return to the Jewish people except through a programme of popular education in Torah, to raise scholarly individuals and to establish fixed periods of study for the general populace. It will not be possible to restore the Jewish people to natural health without a full restoration of its spiritual characteristic, one aspect of which is the fear of sin, a recoiling from it and a turning to prescribed penitence. As the people's vitality is strengthened in all its aspects, there will come an end to the maddening restlessness and our national institutions will resume their concern with reasserting the unique natural interest in morality among the Jewish people.

('The Lights of Penitence')

LEO BAECK
MORAL WITNESS
1873–1956, GERMANY

*Men belong to the realm of the State and to the realm of
God. Which law shall they obey when a conflict occurs?
The hour may come when one is forced to opt for the
temporal or the eternal.
To opt [for the eternal] means to be ready to be a martyr,
to recognize the primacy of religion and its commandments,
its primacy in everything.*

(LEO BAECK, 1925)

When Hitler came to power, the leading Reform rabbi in Berlin, Leo Baeck, was
called to the presidency of the representative body of German Jewry and became
the spokesman for all Jews against the evils of the Nazi regime. In the spirit of
Abravanel and Akiva, Baeck proclaimed the dignity of
Judaism, its people's contributions to society and
the self-worth of the Jewish people. Already a
thinker of international repute – Baeck's major
work, *The Essence of Judaism*, was published in
1905 – and as a faculty member at Berlin's
Hochschule fuer die Wissenschaft des Judentums,
Baeck was encouraged to leave Germany and was
offered prestigious posts in American universities.
He opted to remain with his people, preaching and
writing against the calumnies pronounced by the
Nazis. His bold Yom Kippur prayer, composed in
1935 and distributed to all the synagogues in

Germany, was banned by the Nazis and caused his arrest by the Gestapo. As they were to do on four subsequent occasions, however, the authorities eventually succumbed to the immense international respect in which Baeck was held and released him.

In January 1943, at the age of seventy, Baeck was finally transported to the concentration camp at Theresienstadt. By day he was assigned the menial task of pulling the manure cart, but by night he became the 'teacher of Theresienstadt'. He gave lectures on classical studies and rabbinic literature so that his fellow internees might continue to learn and, by doing so, hold on to hope in their despair. To be caught teaching in the camp was punishable by death, yet hundreds thronged to Baeck's lectures to listen to his lone voice in the darkness, reminding them of the strength and great purpose of humanity at its best. In these short hours of 'freedom', Baeck's listeners were able to forget their imprisonment and the Nazi attempt at subjugation was temporarily defeated.

In May 1945, Baeck was freed by the Allies. His release came as a vindication of the principle he had taught for so long: the absolute imperative of combating evil by becoming an exemplar for good. As the leader of German Jewry in its darkest hour, he stood out as a civilizing influence amidst the horrors of barbarity, and sought to inspire all with his belief in humanity and the universal teachings of Judaism. His life and his work are an enduring testimony to the best that we can be.

FAITH AT THE DARKEST HOUR
In this hour all Israel stands before God, the judge and the forgiver.
In his presence let us all examine our ways, our deeds and what we
*   have failed to do.*
Where we transgressed, let us openly confess:
'We have sinned!' and, determined to return to God, let us pray:
'Forgive us.'

We stand before our God.

With the same fervour with which we confess our sins, the sins of the
individual and the sins of the community, do we, in indignation
and abhorrence, express our contempt for the lies concerning us
and the defamation of our religion and its testimonies.

We have trust in our faith and its future.

Who made known to the world the mystery of the Eternal,
the One God?

Who imparted to the world the comprehension of purity of conduct
and purity of family life?

Who taught the world respect for man, created in the image of God?

Who spoke of the Commandments of righteousness, of social justice?

In all this we see manifest the spirit of the prophets, the divine
revelation to the Jewish people. It grew out of our Judaism and it
is still growing. By these facts we repel the insults flung at us.

(Communal Prayer written for Yom Kippur, 1935, later banned by the Nazis)

THE HUMAN SPIRIT

The prophets turned against every misdeed of history that seeks its
vindication in the success of expediency. They turned against the sort
of politics that creates its own moral code, they objected to any
justification of right by victory. Justice is the ultimate sense of
history for Jewish historiography. If right were to fail there would no
longer be any sense in dwelling on earth. For living means living for
justice, goodness and truth; true history is the history of the spirit,
the human spirit which may at times seem powerless, but ultimately
is yet superior and survives because even if it has not got the might,
it still possesses the power, the power that can never cease.

('Survival' address, Theresienstadt concentration camp, 15 June 1944)

FINDING FREEDOM IN SLAVERY

Here the mass submerged the individual. He was enclosed in the mass, just as he was encircled by the crowded narrowness, by the dust and the dirt, by the teeming myriads of the insects and encircled also by the need and the distress and the hunger that seemed never to end – enclosed in the camp of the concentrated, never alone by himself. Each had received his transport number. That was now his characteristic feature, it was the first and most important sign of his existence. It officially ousted his name and it threatened inwardly to oust his self. That was the mental fight everyone had to keep up, to see in himself and in his fellow man not only a transport number. It was the fight for the name, one's own and the other's, the fight for individuality, the secret being, one's own and the other's. Much, perhaps everything, depended on whether one stood this test, that the individual in one remained alive as an individual and continued to recognize the individual in the other.

('LIFE IN A CONCENTRATION CAMP', MARCH 1946)

LILY MONTAGU
GOD'S SERVANT
1873–1963, ENGLAND

I would venture to suggest that the only hope that we may influence others lies in the strength of our personal religion. If that is real and effective, it may here and there, be our lovely privilege to kindle with the light of our enthusiasm, some other wavering, seeking soul.

(SERMON DELIVERED AT THE WORLD UNION FOR PROGRESSIVE JUDAISM, BERLIN, 1928)

Lily Montagu was born into a distinguished family of Orthodox Anglo-Jews. She had little formal education but built on an instinctive spiritual awareness through reading and discussion with the Anglo-Jewish scholars of the time, including the great theologian and author Claude Montefiore. Montagu's disciplined self-education and exposure to local politics – a heady mix of workers' strikes, campaigns for women's rights and socialist and unionist activities – led her to question the relevance of the Judaism she had been brought up with, especially for working people and their families. Developing a growing uneasiness with Orthodoxy's elaborate but, in her view, superficial ceremonies, she began to look instead for what she described as 'true' religion: a deeply personal force coupled with a humanitarian outlook – a new Judaism that would combine the best of tradition with modern concerns.

In 1899, Montagu published a controversial article entitled 'The Spiritual Possibilities of Judaism Today', drawing attention to the spiritual malaise she perceived in Anglo-Jewry. Her forthright critique attracted much comment and debate, and prompted the formation of the Jewish Religious Union in 1902. Intended to unite all Judaism's denominations in a common goal of strengthened religious life, the Union initially attracted backing from both Orthodox Jews and

British Reform Jews (similar to the Conservative movement in the United States), but was ultimately rejected by Orthodox rabbis because it promoted the equality of women and the use of English prayers. The result was the emergence of the Liberal Jewish movement in Britain (similar to the Reform movement in the United States), based on the ethical and spiritual principles espoused by Montagu and her long-time friend Montefiore.

Montagu became spiritual leader of the West Central Liberal Synagogue in London, and remained committed to the Union (later renamed the Union of Liberal and Progressive Synagogues) for the rest of her life. Her para-rabbinic role was formalized in 1944 when she was inducted as a 'lay minister', the first woman in Judaism ever to be recognized in this way. Always mindful of religion's role in community and social life, she also organized religious services on Sabbath afternoons for young working women, who were either unwilling to attend the synagogue or unable to because of the commitments of home and work.

Montagu possessed an indefatigable spirit and an unshakeable faith. She believed that God has given each of us a task and that, just as the ancient prophets did in their time, it was her duty to respond to that calling. As a woman of her generation, she understood her call to a life of voluntary service, working for the Jewish community, working-class women and the needs of the poor. She died at the age of eighty-nine after a lifetime of pioneering achievements, still writing and preaching on the themes of God's call, true religion and a 'living Judaism'.

RELIGIOUS LIFE

If we examine our Judaism with a trusting spirit, we find that it contains the germs of life. We find that its abiding essence is simplicity and truth. At present our thinkers are oppressed by the religious lethargy from which our age is just emerging. Let us dare to speak with courage to our brothers and sisters and to our sons and daughters. Let us bid them not hesitate in their search after the divine because they use data and methods not already tried by their ancestors. Judaism is strong enough and wide enough to inspire them and their children forever. Let us ask them to make progressive demands upon it. Let us tell them indeed that they can only be Jews and Jewesses if they do live up to the ideals of truth and morality expounded by the best teachers of their age.

('The Spiritual Possibilities of Judaism Today', Jewish Quarterly Review, January 1899)

HERE AM I: SEND ME

It is important that you and I, in our humble way, even as Isaiah did, in his great way, recognize that we have work to do through our affiliation with the community and that work is part of God's charge to each of his children. Like Isaiah, we recognize our limitations and our weaknesses. Even as we dare to say these words: 'Here am I: send me,' we know ourselves to be unworthy of our glorious privileges. But this very knowledge, painful though it may be, is at the same time immensely stimulating and encouraging. At this moment, we are what we are, but in contact with God, our Teacher and Friend, our Master and Leader, we can each become a true servant. We can feel our kinship with God, and let it raise us to new heights and infinite possibilities. 'You shall be holy for the Eternal Your God is holy'
(Isaiah 6:9).

(Sermon, Liberal Jewish Synagogue, June 1944)

THE SPIRIT OF RELIGION

*It seems to me that a beautiful symbol is an aid to holiness. I do not,
you see, feel impelled to follow any observance as my orthodox co-
religionists do, because they regard it as one of the Pentateuchal
Commandments. The test for all outward observances is simply this,
according to my beliefs: does it help me to lead a holier life? Since
we are made up of body and spirit, I think many of us are helped by
outward symbols. Their observance must not be regarded as an end
in itself but as a help to stimulate the spiritual life of the Jew.
Moreover we must not forget that the fellowship between Jews
strengthens their sense of dedication. As a brotherhood, they are
called upon to serve as holy witnesses to the reality of God. Their
spiritual life is all-important and, as I have said, the observances are
quite secondary, but there is a bond between people who love the
same externalities even as they are brought together by sharing the
gifts of the spirit.*

(ERIC CONRAD, 'IN MEMORY OF LILY H. MONTAGU: SOME EXTRACTS FROM HER LETTERS AND ADDRESSES')

AUTONOMY IN RELIGIOUS LIFE

*We could of course be saved from much suffering if God interfered in
human life and stopped us from falling into error or from acting
perversely and perpetrating cruelty. But the God of the Universe
allows freedom of development to his children. Having placed eternity
in our hearts and given us the urge to self-realization, having planted
the seed of divinity in our souls so that they have kinship with him, in
whose image we were created, God leaves to the individual power over
his own life.*

(ERIC CONRAD, 'IN MEMORY OF LILY H. MONTAGU: SOME EXTRACTS FROM HER LETTERS AND ADDRESSES')

STEPHEN S. WISE
CHAMPION OF JUSTICE
1874–1949, UNITED STATES

I am an American Jew who proudly recalls that on the
Independence Bell is inscribed the words from
the Hebrew Bible, 'And you shall proclaim liberty
throughout the land to all its inhabitants...'
So I shall live and labor to the end that all be set free,
and that this spirit rule over all the sons and
daughters of humanity.

('As I See It')

Stephen S. Wise is the perfect example of a modern prophet. Renowned for his impassioned oratory, he became the voice of America's social conscience as he preached the biblical messages of social equality, social welfare and humanitarianism. He never flinched from challenging the public figures of his day, but held to the vision of a just society as his only goal, regardless of the upheaval and controversies he would cause.

Wise was brought to America from Budapest at the age of two. On completion of his education, he became a rabbi in Portland, Oregon, and launched his career as a social reformer by heading a successful campaign for child labour laws. Liberal and outspoken, he soon rose in prominence as a writer and speaker. He helped found numerous Jewish national institutions, including the Jewish Institute of Religion (now joined with the Hebrew Union College as the Reform movement's seminary), the American Jewish Congress and the Zionist Organization of America. As an ardent advocate of democratic principles and human rights, he also helped found non-Jewish national organizations such as the National Association for the Advancement of Colored People and the American Civil Liberties Union.

When Wise was interviewed in the early 1900s for the prestigious rabbinical position at Temple Emanu-El in New York, he let it be known that he would only accept if he were allowed complete freedom in the pulpit – in its day a radical request that was predictably denied. His solution was to establish the Free Synagogue in New York City in 1907. Unfettered by constraints, he used this platform to preach his liberal radicalism, speaking out in particular for the rights of workers and the unemployed – notably, and controversially, defending the rights of the steelworkers to unionize and strike in 1919.

Although successful in his social campaigns, Wise was pessimistic about the prospect of universal peace. An early supporter of the League of Nations, he recognized the need to fight oppression and the evil of Nazi Germany. To this end, he organized a mass demonstration at Madison Square Gardens in New York in 1933 to draw attention to Nazi anti-Semitism and persecution. He hounded politicians and fellow Jews, demanding that they speak out against Fascism, and pleaded passionately but without success with President Roosevelt to give protection to the Jews of Europe. He died in 1949, after witnessing Nazism's final defeat and – rising from the ashes of the Holocaust – Israel's re-establishment as the Jewish homeland after two millennia.

PROPHETIC WARNING

The American Jewish Congress has called but not caused this protest meeting tonight. The American Jewish Congress has not aroused this protest against anti-Jewish wrongs in Germany but has brought within the bounds of law and order an oceanic tide of indignation against the outrages inflicted upon Jews in these days under the Nazi government. Not out of the bitterness of anger but out of the deepest sorrow and the spirit of compassion do we speak tonight. No wrong under the heavens could be greater than to make German Jews scapegoats because Germany has grievances against the nations. We who would secure justice from the nations for Germany and justice to Jews from Germany affirm tonight that Germany cannot hope to secure justice through injustice to its Jewish people. We affirm certain elementary axioms of civilisation: the immediate cessation of anti-Semitic activities and propaganda in Germany, including an end to the policy of racial discrimination and of economic exclusion of Jews from the life of Germany. That is, Jewish life and the human rights of Jews must be safeguarded. Hear the words of a great English statesman [Oliver Cromwell], of one who did as much as any other Englishman of his day to make England mighty: 'Providence would deal good or ill fortune to nations according to how they dealt well or ill by the Jews.' This is not a warning but a prophecy. May the German people merit fulfilment of this prophecy of good fortune by dealing well and justly and as a Christian nation by the Jews.

(RALLY SPEECH, MADISON SQUARE GARDENS, NEW YORK, 27 MARCH 1933)

MARTIN BUBER
PHILOSOPHER OF HOLY DIALOGUE
1878–1965, ISRAEL

The prophets of Israel do not warn against something which will happen in any case, but against that which will happen if those who are called upon to turn, do not.

('THE TWO FOCI OF THE JEWISH SOUL, ISRAEL AND THE WORLD')

According to the philosopher Martin Buber, humans relate to each other and the world around them in two ways: either through *I–It* relationships or through *I–Thou* relationships. To engage with the world on an everyday level, we develop the *I–It* relationship, which allows us a perspective of objectivity and detachment – but to be fully human, we must also engage in *I–Thou* relationships: intimate and mutual connections, which often involve a powerful encounter. Buber explained the *I–Thou* relationship as a 'dialogue', since it entails both parties responding to each other, without losing anything of themselves. He took this further by teaching that humans can encounter God through a similar dialogue: the *I–Eternal Thou* relationship. For Buber, the Hebrew Bible stands as a record of the *Eternal Thou* relationship between God and the Jews – and reading the Bible therefore enables us to enter into a dialogue with God. His criticism of formal religion was that it distracts from a search for God through the dialogue of an open relationship.

Two years after setting out this theory in his famous book, *I and Thou* (1923), Buber was appointed professor of Jewish Religion and Ethics at the University of Frankfurt. As anti-Jewish legislation grew under the Nazis, he also took on the directorship of Jewish Adult Education in Germany, and travelled all over the country teaching, lecturing – often to students who were no longer allowed university entry – and encouraging Jewish identity and self-worth in the face of Nazi persecution and bigotry. His effect was so empowering and his popularity so threatening that, in 1935, he was forbidden to speak in public by the German government.

Buber maintained that a Jew should only follow those Commandments that he or she feels personally bound to observe in their individual relationship with God. This radical position placed him in conflict with traditional Judaism, which considers the teachings of the Torah to be absolutes, not personal preferences. However, Buber's philosophy had a great impact on Christian theologians who sought faith through direct spiritual connection. He argued that faith is not assent to religious traditions or doctrines, but rather an orientation, and an acknowledgement of the presence of God in all relationships. Buber witnessed the horror of Nazi Germany and the tragic conflict surrounding the birth of the state of Israel, but he continued to affirm Moses' teaching that evil is the turning away from the other and the withdrawal from dialogue – while good is the presence of relationship and the turning towards God. With the uncompromising attitude of a prophet, he sought out dialogue and relationship with both the Germans after the war and the Arabs in the Middle East.

JUDAISM'S CONTRIBUTION TO CIVILIZATION

At no other time or place has the spirit been served in the human world with such militancy, generation after generation, as it was by the prophets of Israel. Here the men of spirit took it upon themselves to actualise the affirmation of civilization in the reality of the historical hour. Their fight was directed against all those who evaded the duty of actualising the divine truth in the fullness of everyday life but sidestepping into the merely formal, the merely ritual. To fully appreciate

the significance of prophetic religion for mankind and its civilization, we must ask ourselves why it was precisely in Israel that the normative principle voiced its great protest. In answer, we must point to that religious realism peculiar to Israel which has no room for a truth remaining abstract, hovering self-sufficiently above reality, but for which every truth is bound up with a demand which man, the people, Israel are called upon to fulfil integrally on earth. Men, especially the possessors of power and property, naturally resist the demand for the integral fulfilment of divine truth and justice; they therefore try to limit the service of God to the sacral sphere and in all other spheres recognize his authority merely by words and symbols. This is where the prophetic protest sets in.

(ADDRESS TO THE WORLD UNION FOR PROGRESSIVE JUDAISM, LONDON, JULY 1951)

A PHILOSOPHY OF DIALOGUE

I belong to a group of people who from the time Britain conquered Palestine have not ceased to strive for the concluding of genuine peace between Jew and Arab. By a genuine peace we inferred and still infer that both peoples together should

develop the land without the one imposing its will on the other. In view of the international usages of our generation, this appeared to us to be very difficult but not impossible. We were and still are well aware that in this unusual – yes, unprecedented case – it is a

*question of seeking new ways of understanding and cordial
agreement between the two nations. Here again we stood and still
stand under the sway of a Commandment. We could not and cannot
renounce the Jewish claim; something even higher than the life of our
people is bound up with this land, namely, its work and its divine
mission. But we have been and are still convinced that it must be
possible to find some compromise between this claim and the other;
for we love this land and believe in its future and given that such
love and faith are surely present also on the other side as well, a
union in the common service of the land must be within the range of
possibility. Where there is faith and love, a solution may be found
even to what appears to be a tragic contradiction.*

(OPEN LETTER TO MAHATMA GANDHI, 1939)

HUMANITY AS GOD'S PARTNER

*Judaism regards speech as an event which grasps beyond the
existence of mankind and the world. In contradiction to the static of
the idea of logos, the Word appears here in its complete dynamic as
'that which happens'. God's act of creation is speech; but the same is
true of each lived moment. The world is given to the human beings
who perceive it and the life of man is itself a giving and receiving.
The events that occur to human beings are the great and the small,
untranslatable but unmistakable signs of their being addressed; what
they do and fail to do can be an answer or a failure to answer. Thus
the whole history of the world, the hidden, real world history is a
dialogue between God and his creature; a dialogue in which man is a
true legitimate partner who is entitled and empowered to speak his
own independent word out of his own being.*

('THE FAITH OF JUDAISM IN ISRAEL AND THE WORLD')

JANUSZ KORCZAK
PIONEER OF CHILDREN'S RIGHTS

1879–1940 POLAND

I am not here to be loved and admired
But to Act and Love.
It is not the duty of people to help me
But it is my duty to look after the world
And the people in it.

(JANUSZ KORCZAK)

Janusz Korczak was the pseudonym of Dr Henryk Goldszmit, the physician, educator, writer and children's rights campaigner who dedicated his life to Jewish and Catholic orphans in Poland. Korczak's genius lay in his understanding of the needs and concerns of children and their right to be taken seriously as developing human beings. As their advocate, he brought love and compassion to society's most neglected and forsaken, and lobbied for a Declaration of Children's Rights long before any such document was formally drawn up by the Geneva Convention (Convention on the Rights of the Child, 1989).

In 1912, Korczak was appointed director of the Jewish Orphanage in Warsaw, which under his leadership became one of the most enlightened institutions of its kind. Korczak believed that all children are able to reason and make moral judgements, and he pioneered the use of children's councils in the orphanage to make democratic decisions about its operation. Though many orphans came to him from troubled backgrounds, he approached even the most difficult with respect and trust so that they could learn to give these in return.

Korczak set up a second orphanage, for Catholic children, in 1922, and published his most famous children's book shortly afterwards – *King Matt the First*, an allegorical story about a young king who dreams of making a better world for children. After Germany's invasion in 1939, however, Korczak and his Jewish Orphanage were forced to relocate to the Warsaw ghetto. In this diseased and dangerous environment, Korczak set up a children's hospital to care for the sick and dying he found in the street, and risked his life daily to scavenge for food and medicine for the children in his care.

On 6 August 1942, the Nazis ordered all the children in the ghetto on to trains headed for 'resettlement' in Treblinka. Korczak was offered the chance to escape, but he refused to abandon the children. He led two hundred orphans on to the carriages that would take them and him to the gas chambers. The eyewitness descriptions of that last journey are legendary: the children marched with heads held high, singing and holding the flag Korczak had designed for them. Korczak walked at the fore, leading a child in each hand. As he passed, the ghetto police saluted him in recognition of his courageous and noble act.

Korczak taught a new understanding of the needs and rights of the child and called attention to the child within everyone. Like the prophet Akiva, he acted selflessly for the good of all, both in his life and in his martyr's death.

WE LEARN MOST FROM THE CHILD

We demand respect for a pair of bright eyes, a smooth brow and youthful effort and reliance. A new generation is growing up and a new wave is rising.

They are carrying their faults and virtues and we must give them the opportunity to grow up to be better. We cannot win our case by

simply lamenting over bad heredity. We cannot just tell cornflowers to transform themselves into corn. We are not miracle workers, but neither do we want to become charlatans. We are relinquishing our hypocritical longing for perfect children. We demand the following: eliminate hunger, cold, dampness, airlessness, cramped and over-crowded conditions. You yourselves give birth to sick and crippled children and it is you who create the conditions which produce rebellion and pestilence. It is your own thoughtlessness, foolishness and absence of order which are responsible for everything. We ask for respect, if not humility, for snowy, serene, pure, sacred childhood.

('HOW TO LOVE A CHILD')

WHAT CAN I GIVE YOU?

Unfortunately I can give you nothing but these few poor words. I cannot give you God, for you must find Him in quiet contemplation, in your soul. I cannot give you a homeland, for you must find it in your heart. I cannot give you love of Man, for there is no love without forgiveness, and forgiving is something everyone must learn to do on his own. I can give you but one thing only – a longing for a better life; a life of truth and justice; even though it may not exist now, it may come tomorrow. Perhaps this longing will lead you to God, Homeland and Love. Goodbye! Do not forget!

(KORCZAK'S FAREWELL SPEECH TO EACH CHILD ON LEAVING THE ORPHANAGE)

HOW TO BE IN THE PRESENT

A plea on behalf of respect for the here and now, for today. How can we assure life in the future, if we have not yet learned how to live consciously, and responsibly in the present? Do not trample, hold in contempt or sell the future into bondage. Do not stifle it, rush or force it. Respect every single moment, as it will pass and it will never again be repeated.

('HOW TO LOVE A CHILD')

THE EDUCATOR'S HYMN

Be yourself and seek your own path. Know yourself before you attempt to get to know children. Become aware of what you yourself are capable of before you attempt to outline the rights and responsibilities of children. First and foremost you must realize that you too are a child, whom you must first get to know, to bring up and educate. Children are not the people of tomorrow, but are people of today. They have a right to be taken seriously, and to be treated with tenderness and respect, they should be allowed to grow into whoever they were meant to be. The unknown person inside each of them is our hope for the future.

('HOW TO LOVE A CHILD')

DAVID BEN-GURION
BUILDER AND PROTECTOR OF THE JEWISH STATE
1886–1973, ISRAEL

Ours was a tiny nation possessed of a great spirit,
an inspired people that believed in its pioneering mission
to all men, in the mission that had been preached
by the prophets of Israel. This people gave the world
great moral truths and commandments,
the first to see the vision of a new human society.

('THE IMPERATIVES OF THE JEWISH REVOLUTION')

David Gruen, as he was originally named, was taught Hebrew as a child by well-educated Polish parents. Instilled with a love of Zion by their example, and inspired by the work of Theodor Herzl, he moved to Warsaw at the age of eighteen in pursuit of a technical education that would prepare him for work in Palestine. On finding that the quotas for Jews in the colleges were already filled, he channelled his anger into a resolve to help Jews shape their own destiny and bring about the revival of the Jewish nation. He emigrated to Palestine a year later and went to work in the orange groves as an agricultural labourer. Alongside his fellow pioneers, he suffered malaria, hunger and poverty, but he held fast to his dream of reclaiming the land for its dispersed people.

When the British took over Turkey's control of the Middle East at the end of the First World War and pledged to establish a Jewish homeland in Palestine, Ben-Gurion became elected head of the Jewish Agency, the body set up to co-ordinate the interests of the Jewish population. Britain soon reneged on its promise, imposing severe restrictions on Jewish immigration despite the rise of Hitler in Germany and the desperation of Jews to find a safe haven. Ben-Gurion knew that immigration was the only way to help the Jews of Europe and gather sufficient

numbers to form a state. After Hitler's defeat, he called upon his people to fight the British mandate and ordered the illegal immigration of Jews into Palestine, which attracted international sympathy to the Jewish cause when they were forced by the British to return to post-Holocaust Europe.

On 14 May 1948, David Ben-Gurion emerged triumphant as Israel's first Prime Minister. He served two terms, retiring for a period after the first to settle at Kibbutz Sde Boker in the Negev to work again as a labourer on the land he loved so much. As their charismatic leader, he was adored by the people and became affectionately known as *Hazaken*, 'the old man', in deference to his paternal role as builder and protector of the Jewish state. His grave at Sde Boker overlooks the very wilderness from which the ancient Israelites first made their way towards the Promised Land. Although an avowed socialist, Ben-Gurion looked to the Bible as the source and justification for the Jewish state and its re-establishment. Throughout his life it was an inspiration and military guide, and a historic reminder of the fate of those who do not heed God's word.

THE THIRD JEWISH COMMONWEALTH

The land of Israel was the birthplace of the Jewish people. Here their spiritual, religious and national identity was formed. Here they achieved independence and created a culture of national and universal significance. Here they wrote and gave the Bible to the world. Exiled from Palestine, the Jewish people remained faithful to it in all the countries of their dispersion never ceasing to pray and hope for their return and the restoration of their national freedom . . . . The State of Israel will be open to immigration of Jews from all countries of their dispersion, will promote the development of the country for the benefit of all its inhabitants, will be based on the precepts of liberty, justice and peace taught by the Hebrew prophets, will uphold the full social and

political equality of all its citizens, without distinction of race, creed or sex, will guarantee full freedom of conscience, worship, education and culture, will safeguard the sanctity and inviolability of the shrines and Holy Places of all religions and will dedicate itself to the Charter of the United Nations.

('DECLARATION OF INDEPENDENCE', MAY 1948)

A NEW TORAH

The Jewish redemption is here and it is now. We are very privileged to live at a time when we are not forced to survive culturally on mysticism and dreams. It is not next year in Jerusalem but today. And I am sure that as we are home again, we shall once more be creative as a people. We have already begun to be so. Today we are in the process of writing a new Torah not only with scribes but also with pioneers and farmers, artists and scientists, architects and engineers, legislators and collectivists, citizens in every walk of life. All speak the language of Moses and even the freethinkers among them study deeply in the Book, the source of inspiration, provider of a past and of a vision for the future. Our new Torah is being written now but its best chapters are still to come.

('THE BIBLE IS OUR MANDATE', PRESENTATION TO THE BRITISH ROYAL [PEEL] COMMISSION, 1936)

THE MISSION OF THE PEOPLE

All those who relied upon the great mighty strength of Babylon and Egypt, of Greece and Rome have been forgotten and every trace of them has disappeared. The words and prophecies of those who kept faith with Israel, poor and weak, though have endured down to our own day and have left their imprint on all civilization. It is this orientation of a weak but independent power, the belief in its mission

and its uniqueness that has sustained the Jewish people and brought us to this point. Even in our times, if we have accomplished anything in our homeland, and we have accomplished something, our achievements were made possible by the faith we had in ourselves. The ingathering of the exiles into a socialist Jewish state is, in fact, only a precondition of the fulfilment of the real mission of our people. We must first break the constricting chains of national and class oppression and become free men enjoying complete individual and national independence on the soil of a redeemed homeland. After that, we can address ourselves to the great mission of man on this earth, to master the forces of nature and to develop his unique creative genius to the highest degree.

('The Imperatives of the Jewish Revolution')

ISRAEL AND ITS NEIGHBOURS

We have no conflict with the Arab people. On the contrary, it is our deep conviction that historically the interests and aspirations of the Jewish and Arab peoples are compatible and complementary. What we are doing in our country, in Palestine, is reclaiming the land, increasing the yield of the soil, developing modern agriculture and industry, science and art, raising the dignity of labour, insuring women's status of equality, increasing men's mastery over nature and working out a new civilization, based on human equality, freedom and cooperation in a world which we believe is as necessary and beneficial for our Arab neighbours as ourselves. A Jewish-Arab partnership based on equality and mutual assistance will help bring about the regeneration of the entire Middle East.

(The Jewish Agency before the United Nations,

12 May 1947)

ABRAHAM JOSHUA HESCHEL

SEEKER OF JUSTICE AND HOLINESS

1907–1972, UNITED STATES

For many of us the march from Selma to Montgomery
was about protest and prayer. Legs are not lips and
walking is not kneeling. And yet our legs uttered songs.
Even without words, our march was worship.
I felt my legs were praying.

(RECOLLECTION OF THE MARCH FOR CIVIL RIGHTS, SELMA, ALABAMA, 1965)

As the descendant of a long line of illustrious Polish Hasidic leaders, the child prodigy Abraham Joshua Heschel was fully expected to become a *rebbe*. Doubtless anticipating this himself, he studied at the Talmudic academy in Warsaw, but later found himself drawn to the intellectual ideas of modern civilization, and left Poland for Berlin in the 1930s to pursue a doctoral thesis on the prophets. He did much to bridge the growing divide between Jewish piety and Western academic thought by highlighting the importance of the prophetic critique of social injustice, as well as the prophets' religious experience as God's messengers. He argued that God is not remote, nor simply a commanding voice, but that *God* [is] *in Search of Man* (the title of Heschel's 1955 book) and a very real presence in all our lives.

In 1939, Heschel fled from Nazi Germany to the United States, where he eventually became Professor of Jewish Ethics and Mysticism at the Jewish Theological Seminary in New York. Believing that God and humanity meet in the human deed, he became closely involved in the issues of his time – Vietnam, civil rights, racism, poverty, Soviet Jewry and Israel. Heschel's was a commanding voice and, just as Amos had done before him, he spoke out powerfully on behalf of the marginalized and disenfranchised. In his own words, 'the opposite of good is not evil, the opposite of good is indifference': a conviction that was translated into the political comment, 'In a free society, some are guilty but all are responsible.' It was this credo that prompted Heschel to object so vociferously to the war in Vietnam.

Heschel was one of the twentieth century's greatest religious leaders, hailed by many as a new prophet of Israel. He carried the Torah alongside Martin Luther King on the civil rights marches in the 1960s, thereby implanting an enduring image of a modern Exodus from slavery; he played a major role in the work of Vatican II, challenging the Catholic Church's understanding of its relationship with Judaism; and he was one of the first to focus attention on the plight of Soviet Jews and demand their right to emigrate. He lost so much of his past and culture in the Holocaust, yet he never lost his sense of the divine mystery, thanks in part to his Hasidic background. His writings have a simplicity and poetry that reflect his view of the world as a wondrous universe replete with God, to which humanity's only appropriate response can be song and praise, amazement and joy.

THE MEANING OF THE HOUR

The mark of Cain in the face of man has come to overshadow the likeness of God. There has never been so much guilt and distress, agony and terror. At no time has the earth been so soaked with blood. Fellowmen turned out to be evil ghosts, monstrous and weird. Ashamed and dismayed, we ask, who is responsible? The conscience of the world was destroyed by those who were wont to blame others rather than themselves. Let us remember, we revered the instincts but distrusted the prophets. We laboured to perfect engines and let our inner life go to wreck. We ridiculed superstition until we lost the ability to believe. We have helped to extinguish the light our fathers had kindled. We have bartered holiness for convenience, loyalty for success, love for power, wisdom for information, tradition for fashion.

(THE 'MEANING OF THE HOUR' SPEECH, MARCH, GERMANY, 1938)

LEAP OF ACTION

A Jew is asked to take a leap of action rather than a leap of thought. He is asked to surpass his needs, to do more than he understands in order to understand more than he does. In carrying out the word of the Torah he is ushered into the presence of spiritual meaning. Through the ecstasy of deeds, he learns to be certain of the hereness of God. Right living is a way to right thinking.

('GOD IN SEARCH OF MAN')

LIFE AS A WORK OF ART

Let them remember that there is meaning beyond absurdity. Let them be sure that every deed counts, that every word has power, and that all we can do is our share to redeem the world, in spite of all the absurdities and all the frustrations and disappointments. And above all let them remember to build a life as if it were a work of art. You're not a machine. And you are young. Start working on this great work of art called your own existence.

(NBC TELEVISION INTERVIEW, NEW YORK, 1972)

PROPHETS TODAY

Where does God dwell in America today? Is God at home with those who are complacent, indifferent to other people's agony, devoid of mercy? Is God not rather with the poor and the contrite in the slums? Where in America do we hear a voice like the sound of the prophets of Israel? Martin Luther King is a sign that God has not forsaken the United States of America. Martin Luther King is a voice, a vision and a way. I call upon every Jew to hearken to his voice, to share his vision and to follow his way. The whole future of America will depend upon the impact and the influence of Dr King.

(INTRODUCING MARTIN LUTHER KING TO THE RABBINICAL ASSOCIATION, 25 MARCH 1968)

NOTES TO THE ILLUSTRATIONS

Compiled by Ilana Tahan, Curator of the Hebrew Section of the British Library

Cover
Details from pages 79 and 20.

(p. 12) BL MS Sloane 3173, f. 17 v, 1740
The revelation at Mount Sinai. Kneeling at the top of the mountain, Moses holds up the tablets of the law, while below, the waiting Israelites look away in awe. Surrounded by layers of clouds and radiating beams of light, a central orb contains the Hebrew word *Anokhi* ('I am [the Lord]').

(p. 15) BL MS Add. 27210, f. 10 v (detail), *c.* 1320
The young Moses approaches the burning bush and lifts his covered hand to hide his face, illustrating the verse 'and Moses hid his face for he was afraid to look at God' (Exodus 3:6).

(p. 18) BL MS Sloane 3173, f. 36 v, 1740
Appearing from a cloud, the hand of God sets the tablets containing the Ten Commandments firmly on the ground. The sanctity of the scene is heightened by the bareness of the landscape. According to legend, the Torah was given in the wilderness in a place to which no one had any claim, so that all the world's inhabitants could hear it and accept it.

(p. 20) BL MS Add. 27210, f. 15 r, *c.* 1320
Holding a rectangular timbrel decorated with curlicues, Miriam the prophetess is joined by four maidens playing a lute, a tambourine, cymbals and sticks. On the right, two girls are dancing. The maidens' movements, expressive gestures and elegantly draped clothes typify the French-Gothic style.

(p. 23) BL MS Add. 15282, f. 179 v (detail), *c.* 1300
This standard-bearing, armour-clad soldier represents the leading tribe of Dan. The Hebrew name Dan is derived from the root *dyn* denoting to judge or vindicate. From an illumination preceding the book of Numbers which describes the arrangement of the twelve tribes of Israel into four camps.

(p. 29) BL MS Or. 2626, f. 7 r (detail), 1482
Ornamental square Sephardi script drawn on a filigree and arabesques ground, spelling *Ishah ki tazri'a*, one of the 613 biblical commandments concerning the ritual purity of women laying-in after childbirth.

(p. 36) BL MS Add. 19776, f. 54 v (detail), 1395
A popular motif in Jewish art, the lion has national associations – the tribe of Judah was called a 'lion's whelp' – and is particularly linked to the royal House of David. Lions were among the animals placed on the steps leading to Solomon's magnificent throne of judgement. According to legend, their roaring during a trial would frighten the witnesses, thus preventing them from giving false evidence.

(p. 37) BL MS Or. 2627, f. 258 r (detail), 1482
The opening words from the book of Micah, *Devar Adonai* ('The Word of the Lord'), from the *Lisbon Bible*, one of the most accomplished Hebrew manuscripts, produced in Portugal towards the end of the fifteenth century. The words are written in burnished gold on a mauve lacy surface.

(p. 38) BL MS Or. 2627, f. 258 r, 1482
The frontispiece of the book of Micah in the *Lisbon Bible*. The text, in beautiful Sephardi calligraphy, is surrounded by elegant floral borders pointing to Italian and Flemish influences.

(p. 42) BL MS Harley 5711, f. 31 r (detail), *c.* 1300
An ornamental panel containing *Divre* – the opening word of the book of Jeremiah, copied in Ashkenazi square script. From a Hebrew Bible written and decorated in Italy at the beginning of the thirteenth century.

(p. 43) BL MS Add. 11639, f. 260 r, (detail), *c.* 1280
In a dark cave situated under a crenellated city wall and flanked by a medieval gate, Daniel, the man of God, is kneeling in prayer between two lions. From the *North French Miscellany*.

(p. 46) BL MS Or. 2737, f. 68 r, *c.* 1300
Moses and Aaron in a brotherly embrace. From a *Passover Haggadah* produced in Castile.

(p. 53) BL MS Add. 14761, f. 54 r (detail), *c.* 1340–50
In an arched study, seated in front of a lectern, is the learned Rabbi Akiva, one of the foremost Jewish scholars of the second century.

(p. 54) BL MS Or. 1404, f. 15 r (detail), *c.* 1350–75
This illustration of Rabbi Akiva shows marked Byzantine influence in the facial expressions and posture of the figure. From the *Brother Haggadah*, Catalonia.

(p. 56) BL MS Sloane 3173, f. 27 r, 1740
Clothed in magnificent finery, King David kneels in prayer. The harp leaning against the table and the book of Psalms open in front of him allude to his fame as a musician and psalmist. The scene is imbued with divine light emanating from a bright orb which contains the words *Ruah ha-kodesh* ('the Holy Spirit').

(p. 60) BL MS Add. 11639, f. 116 r, *c.* 1280
King Solomon reading *Torat Mosheh*, a codex of the Pentateuch. The accomplished skill of the artist is manifest in the graceful posture of the king's figure, his subtle facial expression and elegantly draped robes.

(p. 66) BL MS Add. 26968, f. 139 v, 1383
Synagogue scene from an Italian *Siddur*, a prayer book copied and illuminated by Moses ben Yekutiel Hefetz Tsifroni, at Forli. Worshippers recite prayers while the Torah scroll is taken out of the Ark.

(p. 69) BL MS Sloane 3173, f. 35 r, 1740
Moses receiving the Tablets of the Law on Mount Sinai. The bright orb hovering above the mountain, with word *Anokhi* inscribed inside, symbolizes God's omnipresence.

(p. 72) BL MS Sloane 3173, f. 35 v, 1740
The four matriarchs of Israel – Sarah, Rebecca, Rachel and Leah – engaged in a theological discussion on the contents of the books placed in front of them. From a *Passover Haggadah*, written and decorated by Joseph Leipnick, Altona.

(p. 75) BL MS Add. 27210, f. 10 v (detail), *c.* 1320
An illustration to Exodus 5:1–5, showing Moses and Aaron appearing before Pharaoh and his advisers. Moses, carrying a staff and wearing a blue shawl, faces the enthroned Pharaoh, who sits under a canopy.

(p. 76) BL MS Add. 11639, f. 332 v, *c.* 1280
In Jewish theology the Tree of Life is the symbol of wisdom and of the law. This image, showing the Tree filled with birds, varies from the one presented on page 86, and was probably created by a different artist.

(p. 79) BL MS Sloane 3173, f. 6 v (detail), 1740
In most eighteenth-century Haggadah manuscripts, the Wise Son is represented as a learned man. In this image, created by Joseph Leipnick, he appears as a bearded rabbinical scholar wearing a black cloak and dark hat, holding a large red-bound codex under his left arm.

(p. 82) BL MS Sloane 3173, f. 35 v, 1740
An illustration to the verse *Shishah mi yode'a?* ('Who knows six?') from a hymn recited on Passover Eve, showing an elderly man studying from an open book, most likely a volume of the *Mishnah*. The books on the table and filling the bookcase in the background of the picture point to his scholarly status.

(pp. 83 & 85) BL MS Add. 11639, f. 742 v (details), *c.* 1280
The brazen or copper serpent had formidable healing powers. According to the biblical account, whoever had been bitten by a snake would be healed just by looking at it. A group of men gather around the serpent for healing.

(p. 86) BL MS Add. 11639, f. 122 r, *c.* 1280
Standing in the corners of the panel, each holding a lance, four winged angels guard the Tree of Life.

(pp. 88–90) BL MS Or. 12377R (details), 1680
Jerusalem and other holy places, as featured in an Italian marriage contract.

(p. 92) BL MS Add. 27210, f. 10 v (detail), *c.* 1320
Carrying two babies in her arms, Zipporah, Moses' wife, returns to Egypt on horseback. From the *Golden Haggadah*, a fourteenth-century manuscript famed for its full-page miniatures with patterned gold-leaf background.

(p. 97) BL MS Add. 19776, f. 96 r, 1395
Under an archway surmounted by two red towers, a rabbi wrapped in a prayer shawl is reading from a Torah scroll. From a German Pentateuch, completed at Coburg.

(pp. 102–103) BL MS Add. 11639, f. 121 r (details), *c.* 1280
Judith appearing before Holofernes, executed in typically French-Gothic style. Although excluded from the Hebrew Bible, the book of Judith was apparently a popular theme in Jewish manuscript art. The story, which celebrates the courage of a pious Jewish widow, dates from the Maccabean period and has been traditionally associated with the festival of Hanukah.

(p. 107) BL MS Add. 19776, f. 54 v (detail), 1395
King Solomon, whose wisdom and justice were legendary and who was reputed to be able to converse with the animal kingdom, is seated on a throne shaped like the roof of a building. At his feet are a winged dragon, a lion and a dog holding a flower in his mouth.

(p. 109) BL MS Sloane 3173, f. 35 r, 1740
The monotheistic concept, fundamental to Judaism, is well represented in this illustration to the verse *Ehad mi yode'a?* ('Who knows one?') from a hymn sung on Passover Eve.

(p. 110) BL MS Sloane 3173, f. 35 r, 1740
Dressed in Hasidic garb and wearing furry hats, the rabbinic scholars in this miniature portray the three patriarchs of Israel: Abraham, Isaac and Jacob. From Joseph Leipnick's *Passover Haggadah* from 1740.

(p. 113) BL MS Add. 26968, f. 118 r, 1383
The Haggadah passage 'Rabban Gamliel used to say . . . ' is illustrated here with a medieval school scene. On the right, a teacher lectures to a group of pupils; at the left is a bookcase in which the books, bound with clasps, are stored flat.

(p. 117) BL MS Add. 11639, f. 523 v, *c.* 1280
Full-page miniature executed in a French-Gothic style, capturing the fight between David and Goliath. The boy David, armed with only his shepherd's crook and a sling, challenges the heavily armoured Philistine bearing a lance. The dramatic tension of the scene is dampened by the charmingly drawn rams and dog.

Endpapers
Details from page 20 and 85.